WHEN THEY CALL YOU A TERRORIST

WHEN THEY CALL YOU A TERRORIST

A BLACK LIVES MATTER MEMOIR

patrisse khan-cullors
& asha bandele

CANONGATE

Published in Great Britain in 2018 by Canongate Books Ltd,
14 High Street, Edinburgh EH1 1TE

canongate.co.uk

1

First published in the United States in 2018 by St Martin's Press

The moral right of the author has been asserted

British Library Cataloguing-in-Publication Data
A catalogue record for this book is available on
request from the British Library

ISBN 978 1 78689 302 4
Export ISBN 978 1 78689 303 1

Printed and bound in Great Britain by Clays Ltd, St Ives plc.

For my ancestors, and for my mother, Cherice Simpson; my fathers, Gabriel Brignac and Alton Cullors; for all my siblings; and for my new family, Janaya Khan and Shine Khan-Cullors, this book is from you and for you. Thank you for holding me down and reminding me why I am able to heal. ——PATRISSE

For Nisa and for Aundre and for all of our children, the ones who survive, the ones who do not.

And for Victoria, who deserves the sun, the moon, the stars and Coney Island. And Victoria, who first believed, who has always believed. ——asha

And for the movement that gives us hope, and the families in whose names we serve, we will not stop pushing for a world in which we can raise all of our children in peace and with dignity. ——PATRISSE AND asha

contents

It is our duty to fight for our freedom.
It is our duty to win.
We must love each other and support each other.
We have nothing to lose but our chains.

ASSATA SHAKUR

foreword

BY ANGELA DAVIS

When I first met Patrisse Khan-Cullors, I could not have predicted that within a short period of time she, along with Alicia Garza and Opal Tometi, would become the face of a movement that, under the rubric of "Black Lives Matter," would rapidly reverberate throughout the world. But I could clearly see that Patrisse and her comrades were pushing Black and left, including feminist and queer, movements to a new and more exciting level, as they seriously wrestled with contradictions that had plagued these movements for many generations.

In this memoir, Patrisse generously shares the intimacies of her life and loves, and her unyielding devotion to the cause of freedom. The stories she tells here with asha bandele help us to understand why her approach to organizing and movement building has captured the imaginations of so many. Her story emphasizes the productive intersection of personal

experiences and political resistance. The pivotal story of
her brother's repeated encounters with violence-prone police officers, for example, permits us to better understand
how state violence thrives at the intersection of race and
disability. That Monte—Patrisse's brother—is shot with rubber bullets and charged with terrorism as a routine police
response to a manic episode reveals how readily the charge
of terrorism is deployed within white supremacist institu-
tions. We learn not only about the quotidian nature of state
violence but also about how art and activism can transform
such tragic confrontations into catalysts for greater collective
consciousness and more effective resistance.

When They Call You a Terrorist thus illuminates a life deeply
informed by race, class, gender, sexuality, disability, and religion, at the same time as it highlights the art, poetry, and
indeed also the struggles, such a life can produce. But, of
course, it is not only Patrisse's brother who is called a terrorist. It is Patrisse herself, and her co-workers and comrades—
including Alicia, Opal, and the other organizers and
activists affiliated with the Black Lives Matter network
and movement—whose commitments and achievements are
maligned with the label of terrorism. No white supremacist
purveyor of violence has ever, to my knowledge, been labeled a terrorist by the state. Neither the slayers of Emmett
Till nor the Ku Klux Klan bombers who extinguished the
lives of Carole Robertson, Cynthia Wesley, Denise McNair,
and Addie Mae Collins before they could emerge from girl-
hood were ever charged with terrorism or officially referred
to as terrorists. But in the 1970s, President Richard Nixon

instinctively hurled that label at me, and in 2013 Assata
Shakur was designated by the FBI as one of the world's ten
most dangerous terrorists.

There are many lessons to be gleaned from Patrisse's
memoir, not the least of which have to do with political rhetoric. The very title, *When They Call You a Terrorist,* asks the
reader to engage critically with the rhetoric of terrorism—
not only, for example, the way in which it has occasioned and
justified a global surge in Islamaphobia, and how it has im-
peded thoughtful reflection on the continued occupation of
Palestine, but also how this rhetoric attempts to discredit
anti-racist movements in the United States. At the same time,
racist, misogynist, and transphobic eruptions of violence
continue to be normalized. The seemingly simple phrase
"Black Lives Matter" has disrupted undisputed assumptions
about the logic of equality, justice, and human freedom in the
United States and all over the world. It has encouraged us to
question the capacity of logic—Western logic—to undo the
forces of history, especially the history of colonialism and
slavery. This logic expresses itself through our philosophical
certainties and ideological presuppositions and in our legal
system, which, for example, allows for the incarceration of
disproportionate numbers of black people, immigrants from
the Global South, and people of recent immigrant ancestry,
justifying the structural racism of such practices with refer-
ences to due process and other ostensible legal guarantees of
equality.

Patrisse Khan-Cullors and her comrades within the
Movement for Black Lives, which embraces many more

organizations—including the Black Youth Project 100 and the Dream Defenders in Florida—are helping to produce forward-looking movement approaches that represent the best possibilities for the future of our planet. They call for an inclusiveness that does not sacrifice particularity. They recognize that universal freedom is an ideal best represented not by those who are already at the pinnacle of racial, gender, and class hierarchies but rather by those whose lives are most defined by conditions of unfreedom and by ongoing struggles to extricate themselves from those conditions. This recognition and the vast power of love are at the core of Patrisse's powerful memoir.

PART ONE

ALL THE BONES WE COULD FIND

introduction

WE ARE STARDUST

I write to keep in contact with our ancestors and to spread truth to people.

SONIA SANCHEZ

Days after the elections of 2016, asha sent me a link to a talk by astrophysicist Neil deGrasse Tyson. We have to have hope, she says to me across 3,000 miles, she in Brooklyn, me in Los Angeles. We listen together as Dr. deGrasse Tyson explains that the very atoms and molecules in our bodies are traceable to the crucibles in the centers of stars that once upon a time exploded into gas clouds. And those gas clouds formed other stars and those stars possessed the divine-right mix of properties needed to create not only planets, including our own, but also people, including us, me and her. He is saying that not only are we in the universe, but that the universe is in us. He is saying that we, human beings, are literally made out of stardust.

And I know when I hear Dr. deGrasse Tyson say this that he is telling the truth because I have seen it since I was a child, the magic, the stardust we are, in the lives of the people I come from.

I watched it in the labor of my mother, a Jehovah's Witness and a woman who worked two and sometimes three jobs at a time, keeping other people's children, working the reception desks at gyms, telemarketing, doing anything and everything for 16 hours a day the whole of my childhood in the Van Nuys barrio where we lived. My mother, cocoa brown and smooth, disowned by her family for the children she had as a very young and unmarried woman. My mother, never giving up despite never making a living wage.

I saw it in the thin, brown face of my father, a boy out of Cajun country, a wounded healer, whose addictions were borne of a world that did not love him and told him so not once but constantly. My father, who always came back, who never stopped trying to be a version of himself there were no mirrors for.

And I knew it because I am the thirteenth-generation progeny of a people who survived the hulls of slave ships, survived the chains, the whips, the months laying in their own shit and piss. The human beings legislated as not human beings who watched their names, their languages, their Goddesses and Gods, the arc of their dances and beats of their songs, the majesty of their dreams, their very families snatched up and stolen, disassembled and discarded, and despite this built language and honored God and created movement and upheld love. What could they be but stardust, these people who refused to die, who refused to accept the idea that their lives did not matter, that their children's lives did not matter?

Our foreparents imagined our families out of whole cloth. They imagined each individual one of us. They imagined me. They had to. It is the only way I am here, today, a mother and a wife, a community organizer and Queer, an artist and a dreamer learning to find hope while navigating the shadows of hell even as I know it might have been otherwise.

I was not expected or encouraged to survive. My brothers and little sister, my family—the one I was born into and the one I created—were not expected to survive. We lived a precarious life on the tightrope of poverty bordered at each end with the politics of personal responsibility that Black pastors and then the first Black president preached—they preached that more than they preached a commitment to collective responsibility.

They preached it more than they preached about what it meant to be the world's wealthiest nation and yet the place with extraordinary unemployment, an extraordinary lack of livable wages and an extraordinary disruption of basic opportunity.

And they preached that more than they preached about America having 5 percent of the world's population but 25 percent of its prison population, a population which for a long time included my disabled brother and gentle father who never raised a hand to another human being. And a prison population that, with extraordinary deliberation, today excludes the man who shot and killed a 17-year-old boy who was carrying Skittles and iced tea.

There was a petition that was drafted and circulated all the way to the White House. It said we were terrorists. We, who in response to the killing of that child, said Black Lives Matter. The document gained traction during the first week of July 2016 after a week of protests against the back-to-back police killings of Alton Sterling in Baton Rouge and Philando Castile in Minneapolis. At the end of that week, on July 7, in Dallas, Texas, a sniper opened fire during a Black Lives Matter protest that was populated with mothers and fathers who brought their children along to proclaim: We have a right to live.

The sniper, identified as 25-year-old Micah Johnson, an Army reservist home from Afghanistan, holed up in a building on the campus of El Centro College after killing five police officers and wounding eleven others, including two protesters. And in the early morning hours of July 8, 2016, he became the first individual ever to be blown up by local law enforcement. They used a military-grade bomb against Micah Johnson and programmed a robot to deliver it to him. No jury, no trial. No patience like the patience shown the killers who gunned down nine worshippers in Charleston, or moviegoers in Aurora, Colorado.

Of course, we will never know what his motivations really were and we will never know if he was mentally unstable. We will only know for sure that the single organ-

ization to which he ever belonged was the U.S. Army. And
we will remember that the white men who were mass killers, in Aurora and Charleston, were taken alive and one was
fed fast food on the way to jail. We will remember that most
of the cops who are killed in this nation are killed by white
men who are taken alive.

And we will experience all the ways the ghost of Micah
Johnson will be weaponized against Black Lives Matter, will
be weaponized against me, a tactic from the way back that
has continuously been used against people who challenge
white supremacy. We will remember that Nelson Mandela
remained on the FBI's list of terrorists until 2008.

Even still, the accusation of being a terrorist is devas-
tating, and I allow myself space to cry quietly as I lie in bed
on a Sunday morning listening to a red-faced, hysterical Ru-
dolph Giuliani spit lies about us three days after Dallas.

Like many of the people who embody our movement, I
have lived my life between the twin terrors of poverty and
the police. Coming of age in the drug war climate that was
ratcheted up by Ronald Reagan and then Bill Clinton, the
neighborhood where I lived and loved and the neighborhoods where many of the members of Black Lives Matter
have lived and loved were designated war zones and the
enemy was us.

The fact that more white people have always used and
sold drugs than Black and Brown people and yet when we
close our eyes and think of a drug seller or user the face most
of us see is Black or Brown tells you what you need to know
if you cannot readily imagine how someone can be doing

no harm and yet be harassed by police. Literally breathing while Black became cause for arrest—or worse.

I carry the memory of living under that terror—the terror of knowing that I, or any member of my family, could be killed with impunity—in my blood, my bones, in every step I take.

And yet I was called a terrorist.

The members of our movement are called terrorists.

We—me, Alicia Garza and Opal Tometi—the three women who founded Black Lives Matter, are called terrorists.

We, the people.

We are not terrorists.

I am not a terrorist.

I am Patrisse Marie Khan-Cullors Brignac.

I am a survivor.

I am stardust.

1

COMMUNITY, INTERRUPTED

We knew we couldn't make it illegal to be . . . black, but by getting the public to associate the . . . blacks with heroin . . . and then criminalizing [them] heavily, we could disrupt [their] communities . . . Did we know we were lying? Of course we did.

JOHN EHRLICHMAN, RICHARD M. NIXON'S
NATIONAL DOMESTIC POLICY CHIEF, ON THE
ADMINISTRATION'S POSITION ON BLACK PEOPLE

My mother, Cherice, raises us—my older brothers Paul and Monte, my baby sister Jasmine, and me—on a block that is the main strip in my Van Nuys, California, mostly Mexican neighborhood. We live in one of ten Section 8 apartments in a two-story, tan-colored building where the paint is peeling and where there is a gate that does not close properly and an intercom system that never works.

My mother and I are considered short in our family. She is five feet four inches, and I never get any taller than five feet two. But Jasmine, Paul and Monte are tall people, and by the time she is grown, my little sister will reach six feet. My brothers will also both soar up to well over six feet. They get it from our father, Alton Cullors, a mechanic with big, dark brown hands he uses to work the line at the GM plant in Van Nuys, hands that hold me, hug me and make me feel safe. He smells of gasoline and cars, smells that still make me think of love and snuggles and safety almost three decades on. Alton comes in and out of our home, in and out of our days, depending on how he and Mommy are getting along. By the time I am six, he will leave and never live with us again. But he won't disappear entirely from our lives, and his love won't disappear at all. It lingers, that good Alton Cullors love, inside me, beside me, even now, today.

Where we live is multiracial, although by far the majority of people are Mexican. But there are Korean people and Black people like us, and even one white woman who is morbidly obese and cannot bathe in the tub the apartments in our buildings provide. I watch her sneak down to the dilapidated swimming pool attached to our apartment building, the one I will learn to swim in. Each night when she thinks no one is looking, she bathes in the water, bath soap, washcloth, shampoo and all. She never knows I see her and I never say. Not only because she is an adult and I am a child. But because she is part of who makes us, us.

She is poor and raising her daughter alone. She has a fast kind of mouth that reminds me of the quick-tongued Black women in my own family. She wears muumuus. I miss her presence when she leaves, as she eventually does, like most of our neighbors. Ours is a neighborhood designed to be transient, not a place where roots are meant to take hold, meant to grow into trees that live and live. The only place in my hood to buy groceries is a 7-Eleven. Without it, George's liquor store, the small Mexican and Chinese fast-food spots and the Taco Bell we would have nowhere in our neighborhood to get something to eat or drink.

But less than a mile away is Sherman Oaks, a wealthy white neighborhood with big old houses that have two-car garages, landscaped lawns and swimming pools that look nothing like the untended, postage-stamp-size one behind our apartment building. In Sherman Oaks, there is nothing that does not appear beautiful and well kept. There aren't even apartment buildings.

There are just expansive homes with fancy cars in front of them and parents who leave their houses each morning and drive their kids to school, a phenomenon that catches my eye the first time I see it. Mine is a neighborhood of kids who take the bus to school or walk from the time we are in first grade. Our parents are long gone to work by the time we emerge, little multicolored peepers in the springtime, our fresh brown faces trying to figure out a world we did not make and did not know we had the power to unmake.

My own mother worked 16 hours a day, at two and sometimes three jobs. She never had a career, only labored to pull together enough to make ends meet. Telemarketer, receptionist, domestic support, office cleaner—these were the jobs my mom did and all were vital to us, especially after the Van Nuys GM plant shut down and our family's stability did too, right along with it.

Alton got a series of low-wage jobs that had no insurance, no job security and no way to take care of us, his family, which is why I think, looking back now, he left, and while he visited and was always there, it was never the same again. In the 1980s, when all this was going down, unemployment among Black people, nearly triple that of white people's, was worse in multiple regions of the United States, including where I lived, than it was during the Great Recession of 2008–2009.

Sometimes when we would be hungry, when what was left was Honey Nut Cheerios we put water on to eat because there was no milk and, for a year, no working refrigerator in our home, my mother would lock herself in the bathroom and cuss that man to the heavens: Help me fucking feed our children, Alton. Our. Children. What kind of fucking man are you?

I wasn't supposed to hear those conversations, but I sat on the floor outside the bathroom and listened anyway to the yelling, to the problems, to the growl of my empty six-year-old stomach. Being hungry is the hardest thing, and to this day I have prayers of gratitude for the Black Panthers, who made Breakfast for Children a thing that schools should do. We qualified for free lunch and breakfast, and without them I am almost sure we wouldn't have made it out of childhood alive despite my hardworking parents.

We love each other madly, my brothers, sister and I, and we are raised to look out for each other from the very beginning. Jasmine is the baby, our baby, and we love her up as such, but Paul is the oldest, so he takes charge when Alton moves out. It's his voice I wake up to each morning when it's time to go to school and my mother has left already for one of her jobs. It's Paul who gets us ready, tells us to brush our teeth and Come on, let's go. It's Paul who, when we have the ingredients in the house, makes grilled cheese sandwiches for us for dinner just like Mommy taught him to. It's Paul who says, Go on now, time to go to bed, while Mommy is on her second job, whatever it is.

But it's Monte who plays with me, lets me get away with stuff. Monte is the one with the ginormous heart. He can never *not* feed the stray cats and dogs that wander our streets even when our own food supplies are meager. Monte is the one who scoops up the baby birds that fall from their nests, puts them back in the right place. If I close my eyes right now I am back there with him, watching him ever so gently lift a miniature bird—I don't recall what kind we had in our hood—and put it back into the nest, which sometimes had fallen as well.

But Monte, who is the second oldest, is, unlike Paul, also a step removed from responsibility. At night we curl up and watch TV together when I'm supposed to be sleeping. *Beverly Hills, 90210* is our favorite show, a world of rich white kids and their problems, a world where we, and our problems, do not exist. No police cars circle blocks or people in *90210*, not like in Van Nuys, where they do all day, every day, like hungry hyenas out there on the flatlands. For a long time I see them, the police in their cars, but I do not understand them, what role they play in the neighborhood. They do not speak to us or help guide us across streets. They are never friendly. It is clear not only that they are not our friends, but that they do not like us very much. I try to avoid them, but this is impossible, of course. They are omnipresent. And then there comes a day when they pull up near our apartment building. They block the alleyway along the side of it.

The alleyway is where my brothers hang out with their friends and talk shit, probably about girls and all the things they probably never have done with them. Monte and Paul are 11 and 13 years old and there are no green spaces, no community centers to shoot hoops in, no playgrounds with handball courts, no parks for children to build castles in, so they make the alleyway their secret place and go there to discuss things they do not let me in on. I am the girl. Nine years old, I am the little sister banished behind the broken black wrought-iron gate that tries, but fails, to protect us from the outside world.

It's from behind that gate that I watch the police roll up on my brothers and their friends, not one of whom is over the age of 14 and all of whom are doing absolutely nothing but talking. They throw them up on the wall. They make them pull their shirts up. They make them turn out their pockets. They roughly touch my brothers' bodies, even their privates, while from behind the gate, I watch, frozen. I cannot cry or scream. I cannot breathe and I cannot hear anything. Not the siren that would have been accompanying the swirl of red lights, not the screeching at the boys: Get on the fucking wall! Later, I will be angry with myself: Why didn't I help them?

And later, neither Paul nor Monte will say a word about what happened to them. They will not cry or cuss. They will not make loud although empty threats. They will not discuss it with me, who was a witness, or my mother, who was not. They will not be outraged. They will not say they do not deserve such treatment. Because by the time they hit puberty, neither will my brothers have expected that things could be another way.

They will be silent in the way we often hear of the silence of rape victims. They will be worried, maybe, that no one will believe them. Worried that there's nothing that can be done to fix things, make things better. Whatever goes through their minds after being half stripped in public and having their childhoods flung to the ground and ground into the concrete, we will never speak of this incident or the ones that will follow as Van Nuys becomes ground zero in the war on drugs and the war on gangs, designations that add even more license to police already empowered to do whatever they want to us. Now there are even more ways to make us the enemy, even more ways to make us disappear.

And I will not think of this particular incident until years and years later, when the reports about Mike Brown start flowing out of Ferguson, Missouri, and he is morphed by police and the press from a beloved 18-year-old boy, a boy who was heading to college and a boy who was unarmed, into something like King Kong, an entity swollen, monster-like, that could only be killed with bullets that were shot into the top of his head. Because this is what that cop did to him. He shot bullets into the top of his head as he knelt on the ground with his hands up.

I will think of it again when I watch bike-riding Freddie Gray, just 25, snatched up and thrown into the back of a police van like he was a bag of trash being tossed aside. Freddie Gray, taken for a Baltimore "rough ride" vicious enough for the cops in the case to be charged with depraved heart murder. Those actual words. Cops who would be, like most law enforcement accused of shooting Black people, acquitted. Even with the presence of video.

Soon after the day that my brothers were set upon in the alley by cops, a new cycle begins: they start getting arrested on a regular basis, and it happens so often that my mother is eventually forced to move us to another part of Van Nuys. But there is nowhere that they can be or feel safe. No place where there are jobs. No city, no block, where what they know, all they know, is that their lives matter, that they are loved. We try to make a world and tell them they are impor-tant and tell ourselves we are too. But real life can be an insistent and merciless intruder.

Later, when I am sent out of my neighborhood, to Mil-likan, an all-white middle school in wealthy and beautiful Sherman Oaks, I will make friends with a white girl who, as it turns out, has a brother who is the local drug seller.

He literally has garbage bags filled with weed. *Garbage bags.*

But that surprises me less than the fact that not only has he never been arrested, he's never even feared arrest. When he tells me that, I try to let it sink in, living without fear of the police. But it never does sink in.

2
TWELVE

One of the worst things about racism is what it does to young people.

ALVIN AILEY

The first time I am arrested, I am 12 years old.

One sentence and I am back there, all that little girl fear and humiliation forever settled in me at the cellular level.

It's the break between seventh and eighth grades, and for the first time I have to attend summer school because of my math and science grades and I am angry about it. No other Millikan kids come here, to this school in Van Nuys, for remediation, only me. The summer school I attend is for the kids who live in my neighborhood. It doesn't have a campus, but it has metal detectors and police. There are no police or metal detectors at Millikan.

Somehow, mentally, I don't make the adjustment. I still

think of myself as a student there, which I am but not for these summer months, and one day I do what I'd learned from my Millikan peers to do to cope: I smoke some weed. At Millikan it is a daily occurrence for kids to show up to class high, to light up in the bathroom, to smoke on the campus lawn. No one gets in trouble. Nowhere is there police. Millikan is the middle school where the gifted kids go.

But in my neighborhood school things are totally different and someone must have said something about me and my weed—two girls had come into the bathroom when I'd been in there—because two days later a police officer comes to my class. I remember my stomach dropping the way it does on one of those monster roller-coaster rides at Six Flags. I can just *feel* that they are coming for me and I am right. The cop tells me to come to the front of the room, where he handcuffs me in front of everyone and takes me to the dean's office, where my bag is searched, where I am searched, pockets turned out, shoes checked, just like my brothers in the alleyway when I was nine years old. I have no weed on me but I am made to call my mother at work and tell her what happened, which I do through tears. I didn't do it, Mommy, I lie through genuine tears of fear. My mother believes me. I am the good girl and she takes my side.

Later, when we are home together, she will not ask me how I am feeling or get righteously angry. She will not rub my wrists where the handcuffs pinched them or hold me or tell me she loves me. This is not a judgment of her. My mother is a manager, figuring out how to get herself and her four children through the day alive. That this has happened, but that she and her kids are all at home and, relatively speaking, safe, is a victory for my mother. It is enough. And for all of my childhood, this is just the way it is.

What made middle school such a culture shock, beyond the race and class differences, was that all throughout elementary school I was considered bright, gifted even, a star student whom my fourth-grade teacher, Ms. Goldberg, indulged when I asked if I could teach the class about the Civil Rights Movement. A week before she had given me a book, *The Gold Cadillac* by Mildred Taylor, about a girl making the frightening drive with her father from Ohio through the Jim Crow South, down to Mississippi, where her extended family lives.

The terror in it was palpable for me, the growing sense on every page that they might be killed; by the time I was nine, police had already raided our small apartment in search of one of my favorite uncles, my father Alton's brother. My uncle who used and sold drugs, and who had a big laugh and who used to hug me up and tell me I was brilliant, but who did not with live us, whose whereabouts we did not know the day the police in full riot gear burst in.

Even tiny Jasmine, probably five years old during that raid, was yelled at and told to sit on the couch with me as police tore through our home in a way I would never later see on *Law and Order: Special Victims Unit,* where Olivia Benson is always gentle with the kids. In real life, when I was a little kid, when my brothers and sisters were, we were treated like suspects. We had to make our own gentle, Jasmine and I, holding each other, frozen like I was the day of the alley-way incident, this time cops tearing through our rooms instead of the bodies of my brothers.

They even tore through our drawers. Did they think my uncle was hiding in the dresser drawer?

But as with the incident with my brothers, we did not speak of it once it was over.

In any event, I am sure this incident is at least partially why *The Gold Cadillac,* of another time and another place, was a story I clung to so deeply, why I remember it now, decades on. Where the details wove together differently, the fear drawn out across those pages is the same, is my own. Finishing it, I wanted more. I wanted confirmation that that which we did not speak of was real. Which was why I asked, Please, Ms. Goldberg, may I have more books to read?

Of course, she said, and gave me stories I devoured, child-size bites of the fight for freedom and justice.

Please, I went back and asked Ms. Goldberg, can I teach the class about the books?

Yes, she said, Why not? Because that's how she was. Ms. Goldberg, with her 80s' feathered brown hair and her *Flashdance*-style workout gear she wore to school every day.

I had a reward—pieces of candy—for my classmates who answered the questions I posed during the 15-minute presen-tations I was allowed to give on the books I read. I wanted them to know our history in this nation, what it was we come from. I wanted them to learn, as I had learned, the terror we knew. Somehow it connected to a terror I—we—felt in our own neighborhoods, in our own current lives, but could not quite name.

But between Ms. Goldberg and then Ms. Bilal—the afterschool teacher and the single dark-skinned Black woman I would have during my early education, who brought us Kwanzaa and Afrocentricity—I turned toward middle school hopeful, even if it was in a community I didn't know, a community without my community. I expected to still be loved, encouraged. My best friend Lisa's mother was the one who'd heard of Millikan. It was considered generally a good school, but what made it special was its program for gifted children centered on the arts. She submitted Lisa's name as a candidate and then, Why not, she told my mother and I one afternoon. With your permission, I will submit Patrisse's name too! Great if the girls can stay together, I remember her saying.

Months on, I was accepted to the gifted children's program; Lisa was not. But Lisa's mom was able to manipulate her address and get Lisa into the standard program, so in the end we are both Millikan students. But we don't remain friends, not as we were.

Millikan Middle School is sufficiently far enough away from my home that I need a ride each morning in order to get to school on time. Before, I could simply hop on the city bus with all the other kids from my hood, but getting into Sherman Oaks is a more complicated endeavor. The problem is that my family does not own a car, which is why our neighbor Cynthia steps in to help. My mother borrows her car to ensure my safe passage. This is not quite as straightforward as it may sound.

Cynthia, no more than 19, a young mother who has on and off been involved with my brother Monte and who will eventually have a child, my nephew Chase, with him, had been shot a year before in a drive-by while she was at a party. From the waist down, she was left paralyzed. But she has a car she loans my mother, a beat-up, champagne-colored station wagon. The back windows are gone, replaced by plastic lining, and the whole thing smells like pee because with Cynthia being mostly paralyzed, she sometimes loses control of her bladder.

My mother takes me to Millikan in that car, which initially I deal with because, a car! But after the first day, I realize quickly I have to make a change. Day two and I say, Drop me off here, Mommy, meaning a few blocks away from the school. The car we are in does not look like any of the other cars that pull up to Millikan, all gleaming and new in the morning sun. Kids pour out of those vehicles, Mercedes and Lexuses, and run from waving parents onto the campus's greener-than-green lawn, as all at once I become familiar with a sudden and new feeling taking root in my spirit: a shame that goes deep, that is encompassing and defining. I realize we are poor.

Later, as an adult, a friend will say to me, Of course you felt that. Oppression is embarrassing, she will say quietly. But in middle school, segregated as it is, between Black and white kids, wealthy and poor kids, I don't quite know what to do with this feeling or the terrible question that encircles my 12-year-old soul: Am I supposed to be embarrassed about the people who nurtured me, who gave me to the world and gave the world to me?

I don't fit in with the white kids who smoke weed in between classes in bathrooms or on the campus lawn. I don't fit in with the few Black girls who want to be Janet Jackson or Whitney Houston when they grow up. I wear MC Hammer pants, crotch swinging low. I wear my own brand of Blackness informed as it also is by the Mexicanness of the neighborhood I was raised in. People say I am weird, but I don't feel weird. I only feel like myself: a girl from Van Nuys who loves poetry and reading and, more than anything, dancing. I am in the dance department and my dances are equal parts African, Hip Hop and Mariachi, which is also to say, weird.

I do make a friend, a white boy, Mikie, who is not disturbed by my alleged weirdness, my MC Hammer pants. I pester my mother to allow me to bring him home. I love my room and I want him to see the place I became me. I don't yet appreciate my mother's own shame, the humbleness of our home. My mother who came from middle-class, pious parents who had cast her aside when she turned up 15 and pregnant with my brother Paul nearly two decades before.

Because despite the shame I feel within the walls of Millikan, away from there, it disappears to a large degree. This neighborhood, this world, is all I have known, it's what I have loved, despite the hardship I don't really know as hardship because it's how everyone lives. Everyone is hungry at times. Everyone lives in small, rented apartments. Most of us don't have cars or extra stuff or things that shine.

In any case, my mother relents, probably out of exhaustion, and Mikie, who will become my first boyfriend in the years before he comes out as Gay and me as Queer, is dropped off at my apartment building by his parents.

I go downstairs to let him in and in the background there is an ambulance on the block screeching, which I don't notice at first because there's always an ambulance screeching on the block. But for Mikie it is new and between that and our building with its peeling paint, my friend says matter-of-factly, without trying to be mean, I didn't think you lived like this. I do not respond. We go into my room and try to act as though things are the same.

Middle school is the first time in my life when I feel unsure of myself. No one is calling me gifted anymore. No one, save for my dance teacher, encourages me or seems to have patience with me. It's in middle school that my grades drop for the first time and that I come to believe that maybe all that love I'd gotten in elementary school had somehow dried up, my ration run dry. At the age of 12 I am on my own, no longer in the world as a child, as a small human, innocent and in need of support. I saw it happen to my brothers and now it was happening to me, this moment when we become the thing that's no longer adorable or cherished. The year we become a thing to be discarded.

For my brothers, and especially for Monte, learning that they did not matter, that they were expendable, began in the streets, began while they were hanging out with friends, began while they were literally breathing while Black. The extraordinary presence of police in our communities, a result of a drug war aimed at us, despite our never using or selling drugs more than unpoliced white children, ensured that we all knew this. For us, law enforcement had nothing to do with protecting and serving, but controlling and containing the movement of children who had been labeled super-predators simply by virtue of who they were born to and where they were born, not because they were actually doing anything predatory.

I learned I didn't matter from the very same place that lifted me up, the place I'd found my center and voice: school. And it will not be until I am an adult, determined to achieve a degree in religion, part of a long and dedicated process I undertook to become an ordained minister, that I will enjoy school again.

A few years after I complete my degree, Dr. Monique W. Morris published her groundbreaking book, *Pushout: The Criminalization of Black Girls in Schools*, demonstrating how Black girls are rendered disposable in schools, unwanted, unloved. Twelve percent of us receive at least one suspension during our school careers while our white (girl) counterparts are suspended at a rate of 2 percent. In Wisconsin the rate is actually 21 percent for Black girls but 2 percent for white girls.

But having attended schools with both Black and white girls, one thing I learned quickly is that while we can behave in the same or very similar ways, we are almost never punished similarly. In fact, in white schools, I witnessed an extraordinary amount of drug use compared to what my friends in my neighborhood schools experienced. And yet my friends were the ones policed. My neighborhood friends went to schools where no mass or even singular shootings occurred, but where police in full Kevlar patrolled the hallways, often with drug-sniffing dogs, the very same kind that they turned on children in the South who demanded an end to segregation.

By the time Black Lives Matter is born, we not only know that we have been rendered disposable because of our lived experience—which few listened to—but also from data and finally from those terrible, viral images of Black girls being thrown brutally out of their seats by people who are called School Safety Officers, for the crime of having their phones out in the classroom. Monique Morris's reporting will tell us about the 12-year-old girl from Detroit who is threatened with both expulsion and criminal charges for writing the word "Hi" on her locker door; and the one in Orlando who is also threatened with expulsion from her private school if she doesn't stop wearing her hair natural.

Twelve.

And for me, too, it started the year I turned twelve. That was the year that I learned that being Black and poor defined me more than being bright and hopeful and ready. I had been so ready to learn. So willing.

Twelve, the moment our grades and engagement as students seem to matter less than how we can be proven to be criminals, people to be arrested.

Twelve, and childhood already gone.

Twelve, and being who we are can cost us our lives.

It cost Tamir Rice his life.

He was a child of twelve. And the cop who shot him took under two seconds, literally, to determine that Tamir should die.

Tamir Rice. Twelve.

Twelve, and out of time.

3

BLOODLINES

She did not tell them to clean up their lives or go and sin no more. She did not tell them they were the blessed of the earth, its inheriting meek or its glorybound pure.

She told them that the only grace they could have was the grace they could imagine.

TONI MORRISON

Yet for all the ways that middle school challenges me, for all the culture shock and for all of my struggles with the math and science courses, there is one incident that defines it more than any other, and it has everything to do with police and nothing to do with police and everything to do with poverty and nothing to do with poverty. It has everything to do with being Black and nothing to do with it.

Just before I cross that sixth-grade elementary school stage, just before I head off to Millikan and Sherman Oaks, a confident graduate about to rush headlong into the next chapter of my life, my mother and I are out, shopping for groceries. At some point between the Cheerios being put in the cart and the milk, she turns to me and says, I need to talk to you when we get home. Okay, I say, though I wonder, Why not talk to me now?

At home, after the groceries are put away, she guides me into her bedroom, onto her bed, patting it for me to sit beside her. I do. She takes a deep breath. This is not a conversation that she wants to have. And then she just blurts it out. Alton is not your father, she says. He's Paul's and Monte's and Jasmine's. But in between Monte and Jasmine, we broke up and I fell in love with Gabriel and we had you.

Gabriel? I ask. Do you mean that man who has been calling the house for the last few months?

Yes, she says. Gabriel is your father. It is a statement that makes no sense to me.

Do you want to meet him? she asks.

Her words confuse me. I don't know what to say, what to think. I don't want any of this. In the background my mother is saying something about running into Gabriel, exchanging numbers, her telling him about me. But I barely hear these details. I am in prayer: Can everything be the same? Please, God? Please?

I look at my mother but none of this comes out. I try to

speak but cannot. I pull and pull from a place inside me I
cannot name and then I say, hard and quick, That would be
okay. I want to meet my father.

From the time my mother tells me about Gabriel until I
meet him a month later, there is no conversation about him
in our home. There is no backstory. No this is how we met.
This is how we fell in love. This is where you really come
from. We are a family of survivors and a family of doers, but
we are not a family of talkers. We do not process, my family,
we do not take it all down to the bones of it. Gabriel goes
undiscussed, exists almost like an imagined friend, or else
someone I meet in dreams that are hazy, not quite knowable,
but still present.

But there is this one time, this one conversation. It happens with Alton, the only father I've ever known. Six years
he's been gone from our home. Six years of him visiting
only, and us never knowing when. I am 12 and I will not
connect his disappearance from us to any larger social or
structural disruption but only to the idea that we, the kids,
must have done something wrong to make this big, loving
man go away. I will not know how he had been disappeared
from himself, disappeared from the only life he'd ever
known: 20 years on the line at the GM Van Nuys plant and
then nothing. Alton will find jobs well below his skill set at
garages, but he will never again know stability or a living
wage. And all I will know then is that I love him and I miss
him. Alton with all his big emotion and laughter. Which is

why on this day when he comes through the door, unbidden and loud, and says, Come on girl, let's go get something to eat, I am grateful and bound out behind him. Little shadow follows big shadow.

We walk down the block holding hands. Down past the 7-Eleven where we get our groceries. Down past George's Liquors, where I will one day buy cigarettes. Down to the small hole-in-the-wall, the Mexican spot with the name no one ever seems to remember. We order tacos, but before I can start eating, I look up at Alton, his brown face gleaming with sweat in the Van Nuys sun, and I see them, the tears, they are falling freely, incongruently with a man who looks like he does, all muscle tip-to-tip, a man who started lifting weights when he was 14 years old and never stopped.

Alton and his Jheri curl, his 501 jeans with the super-hard crease down the center, his Stacy Adams shoes. Alton and his 18-pack abs that peek out from the silk shirt he always wears mostly unbuttoned when he isn't working. Alton whose masculinity is ripped from the headlines. His tears push for real.

Am I still your father? he asks.

Of course, I say.

We pause.

And then, about my mother: I didn't want her to tell you, he says. I never wanted you to feel like you were half anything, step nothing. Like you weren't mine. You've always been mine. I didn't want you to feel different.

I cannot figure out how to respond. I have not been prepared for any of this. I only know I do not want to betray him, my Alton, my father. I want him to just feel what my 12-year-old heart, my 12-year-old brain, cannot find the words to say. I wish right then we would simply say I love you a million times but we don't. It isn't what we come from. We say nothing and just eat and are silent. But the tears are a sign. Everything is changing and I feel guilty. It all feels like my fault.

But I have to meet Gabriel.

A month after the conversation in the bedroom with my mother, and three weeks after the tacos and tears with Alton, I meet Gabriel for the first time. We make plans, a date, and I watch out the window until I see him walk up to our broken iron gate. He rings the bell and I am the one who lets him in. I am left breathless when I see him; we look exactly alike.

We don't stay in the apartment long. My mother and he do not hug. She is not a hugger. But they are cordial. After five minutes we leave. We get on the bus and head to the movies, although what we saw is gone forever from my memory.

He does not have a car yet. He rides the bus to see me. We ride the bus to our date. I am awkward with Gabriel the whole time, unsure of what to say, how to act. It makes no difference to him. He hugs and kisses me throughout the day, the way you might do with a newborn baby, which in a way, to him, I am. I accept his affection, but do not return it. I am not yet comfortable with this new father in my life.

Gabriel tells me he lives in a home for sober adults. He

tells me right away he's in recovery from crack addiction. I know about crack. Everybody uses it, it seems like. At least in my neighborhood where there are no playgrounds, no parks, no afterschool programs, no hangout spots, no movie theaters, no jobs, no treatment centers or health care for the mentally ill, like my brother Monte, who had begun smoking crack and selling my mom's things and is already showing signs of what we would much later come to know as schizoaffective disorder.

But without health care beyond LA County USC hospital, we can't know about my brother. We only know that crack filled the empty spaces for a lot of people whose lives have been emptied out. We are the post-Reagan, post–social safety net generation. The welfare reform generation. The swim or motherfucking sink generation. And, unlike our counterparts on Wall Street, where crack is used and sold more, we don't have an employee assistance plan.

Later, when I am home, none of my siblings will ask me how it went. Did I like him? What did we do? I have shared everything with these three people: Monte, Paul and Jasmine. Secrets, fears, rooms, triumphs, disappointments. They all eventually tumble out of us. But not this one. This story is tucked inside a world only I live in.

And then one day after I meet Gabriel, my mom and I get into a terrible argument. I don't recall what I say or do, only that I am angry at everything and everyone and I am talking back to her and she slaps me hard across the face. My brother Paul intervenes immediately. He takes me in his arms and he holds me. It seems like hours. He holds

me and rocks me, my six-foot-two, 180-pound muscle-
bound brother.

You will always be my sister, Paul whispers to me.

You will always be ours, he says.

A week after the movies comes Gabriel's graduation. My
father's graduation. He's been in a Salvation Army drug and
alcohol treatment program. My mother is the one who takes
me to it. We do not speak during the ride, but she has made
sure my face is clean, my clothes are neat. *Her* daughter is
presentable. We arrive at the Salvation Army, which is a
church and also the sober living house where my father re-
sides. My mother and I go to the graduation. I see my father
for the second time. He is one of nearly 20 men who will
be celebrated.

His large, almost unwieldy family—my family now—
have gathered and no sooner does he rush to greet me, to
scoop awkward me up, than so do they. I am awash in their
kisses, their hugs. There are uncles, two of them that day,
and three aunties. My father is one of ten siblings. This is
your grandmother, Gabriel tells. She is small, short like me,
five feet two, and her name is spelled Vina, but it's pro-
nounced Vi-KNEE. I don't know why.

But Grandma Vina comes from Eunice, Louisiana, and
her father was white and her mother was Creole. She—my
new grandma—has long gray hair down to her butt, although she wears it brushed back into a bun. She is wearing sweatpants and sneakers and a t-shirt. I will learn that
she is a Scorpio and that family is everything to her, her

proof of life, of meaning. I will learn she cusses a lot, has a fourth-grade education, and my father was her first son and the first child of her own choice. She had two daughters before him but she didn't raise those girls. I will learn that my aunties Lisa and Barbara were the products of rape.

A white man got her, my father tells me once when I ask why Auntie Lisa and Auntie Barbara always seem so angry.

A white man got Grandma Vina, and she was very young, he says. She couldn't raise them girls. That's all I know, he says, and we never speak of it again. No one does.

These pieces of family history and harm that never heal, that pass on generation to generation.

But I love my new grandma immediately, as soon as she smiles wide as the ocean and says, Well, well. Look at Ms. Brignac, after giving me the biggest hug of all hugs right before Darius, my father's only other child, joins in. He is 20. I am his lost-and-found sister. We look at each other. We pause for a moment. We hug.

My father's family is a cash-poor family, unlike my mother's. My mother's family is middle class. The only reason that we are poor is that my mother got pregnant young, which violated Jehovah's Witness rules, sex outside of marriage and all that. They shun her and for years she will work and work to get accepted back into the Kingdom Hall, back into love. She sort of makes it, eventually, over years, but never in enough time to climb back into middle-class safety.

But my mother's family, my mother's world is nowhere to be found in this Salvation Army, in this church, in the rows and rows and rows of pews. Just this new world and I feel like an astronomer who has suddenly discovered a new planet. But a planet without Paul without Monte without Jasmine without Mom without Alton. A planet without the me who exists alongside the people I live and fight and love with.

I don't know how to sort my feelings, which is why, with no other choice, I set them aside. And soon enough, when I am in the presence of Grandma Vina and my father and my uncles and aunties and Darius, they stop occurring to me. I am officially two Patrisses. My mother's daughter and my father's daughter, which don't quite add up to one whole child.

But on this day, I don't concern myself with that. I listen, instead and intently, as my father gives a speech about having his family back. He talks about healing and he talks about our right to it. As I grow older I will come to question 12-step programs, see their failures, all the ways they do not reduce the harms of addiction by making their harms accrue to the individual, alone. They do not account for all the external factors that exacerbate chaotic drug use, send people into hell. The person who only has alcohol or crack at their fingertips almost never does as well as the person who has those things but also a range of other supports, including the general sense that their life matters.

But what is consistent in this moment—and all the moments that will follow that I am in 12-step rooms—is that I will learn there is something radical and beautiful and deeply transformational in bearing witness to public accountability, accountability before a community gathered for the sake of wholeness.

And on this day, in this hour, my father is humble.

My father apologizes.

Have I ever heard an adult apologize?

Did Alton ever say sorry for leaving us, for us being hungry? Did GM ever apologize to him or the hundreds of others whose lives were entirely disrupted by its closure—with no plan for what they could do next to support themselves and their families, no plan to continue a life with dignity? But here is Gabriel apologetic and public and I have no context for it. My mother is secretive. Ours is a home where grown folks' business is grown folks' business. Gabriel is public. Even in the moments of shame. He always returns to truth and honesty. He talks to the audience but I know he is really talking to me, talking to his family. He praises us. He thanks us for not throwing him away, for staying by his side when he went to prison, which is how our society responded to his drug use.

Later, when I get home no one asks me, How did it go? What was it like? Who else was there? I don't remember any conversation at all, as though there wasn't this whole universe growing just outside our door. I remember going into my room, going to sleep, getting up the next day and heading to school. And everything was everything.

From this point onward, Gabriel is immediately and continually present. After the Salvation Army graduation, he starts picking me up every single Friday and we go to

Grandma Vina's house, where there is always a huge collection of family members. My father's family is a sports family, with football games, college and professional, held up like holy moments. But it doesn't really matter. Football, baseball, basketball, golf for goodness' sake, tennis, hockey. You name it, my uncles had the stats on it. But nothing was like the weekends of football and my Grandma's poor man's gumbo—gumbo without the seafood, only chicken, in it.

Now and again in these moments I think of Paul, Monte and Jasmine—and Alton—whose presence is far less predictable. I wonder, though briefly, what that feels like, to watch me disappear each weekend with my found father. But with no answers, no guide, mostly I just bathe myself in these loud, Southern people who look like me and who dance like me and slowly and slowly, I begin to feel like one of them, feel like a Brignac.

I learn to look forward to things I'd never before considered, like Christmas, Thanksgiving and birthdays. Coming up in the Kingdom Hall meant we never celebrated these things; they're not in the Bible and we took the Bible pretty damn literally. I used to go, as a fourth grader, to school with my Bible and my *Watchtower*. I would read aloud from them to my classmates and I never, never felt like I was missing anything by not celebrating Christmas because being in the Kingdom Hall made me feel special, anointed. But now I am with another group, Catholic people, and they love God and they celebrate and eat food and laugh and cuss, although they don't exchange gifts because who has money for gifts? But the love fills us to overflow.

Eventually, Gabriel, who could always find some low-level job no matter what, gets a car of his own—a gold-colored Lincoln Town Car, and we're really off and running then. He does things my mother never could, my mother with her job piled on job, shift piled on shift. But Gabriel has the time and more, the heart for me and my now early teenage friends. We pack his car with our bodies and our stories and he drives us to movies, to pizza, to wherever our 13-year-old hearts desire. He never tells us we are too loud although surely we are too loud.

But it isn't only movies and friends and family and football. Gabriel is deeply invested in his healing and one day he says, Come on, and we jump in the car and drive into the San Fernando Valley, the real hood part, Pacoima, and we pull up to a church and get out. Come on, my father tells me, and I follow him down into a room where a small group of men are meeting.

There was never a time in my childhood that I can recall when people did not call me an old soul, and maybe that's why my father thought I could handle being in his 12-step meeting. Or maybe because, like me, he always wanted a road dawg with him. But while I remember how overwhelmed I was by men talking about things they'd done that had hurt their families while they were struggling with addiction—their absences from family life was a repeated theme—and I remember my father talking about hiding, how he never wanted his family to see him high, what I recall most thinking about was that the honesty was life-giving. As I attended these meetings over the years and after

I spent time working as an adult counselor myself, I wondered: Why are only individuals held accountable? Where were the supports these men needed? Men talking about broken dreams and no jobs and feeling hated by the world and being beat up by police.

But more than anything in those first years, the meetings make me closer to Gabriel, closer to my father. We go for an hour and I listen to men tell their stories and cry and I watch them hold and support one another and then my father finds some small spot to eat—there was a Filipino place he loved best—and we process his life, our life, what it means to build and be in a relationship together.

I'm not here to take you away from anyone, he tells me more than once. I'm just here to add to your life in a way that's good and useful. I believe him. I lean into him, my spirit does. Children so rarely get to see adults be so honest and open and accountable in a way that is grounded, not reactionary. I could not name it then, how these conversations left me, but they start to change me, begin to commit me to being the same.

Still, it isn't all intense meetings and talk of failures and sobriety. It is also many weekend barbeques at the park where my dad and his brothers play baseball. They'd formed an adult league, uniforms and all, and during the season, we all go and cheer them on and eat. These are the moments I love the most, the moments when the animosity between siblings falls by the wayside, and they only happen when my father is present and well, I am told. When he is absent, the games are, too.

But when he is present, we make time in the park, and the siblings, not all from the same father, come together. The first two girls who hadn't been raised by Grandma Vina, the girls who were children of my grandma's rape, even come. My father is the third child and the first child of her choosing. My grandma had been a mistress and my father was the only baby from that union. The next set of children were born after her marriage to a man no one speaks of anymore, a man who was abusive, physically and emotionally. My Grandma coddles these children, even now, perhaps trying to soothe the wounds their father caused, while Barbara and Lisa seethe in the background, their father the white man, their father the rapist.

When the anger boils over, as it often does, it is Gabriel everyone goes to. Gabriel is Switzerland or maybe the original idea of the UN. He processes with them, pushes them to forgive, to choose love. He uses his thin brown body and his big beautiful heart as salve, as medicine. With Gabriel any one of them, any one of us, can appear unmasked and unafraid and he pulls us close. He tells us he cherishes us. Makes us feel things will settle and be all right. Look at me, he says. He reminds us love wins. And for me, a girl from a home of little verbal expression and even less physical expression, I start to know a freedom I hadn't realized I needed. I start to feel something like home in my own skin and sinew, bones and blood. I want this never to end. To go on and on. To forever be the normal I know. Only nothing is forever.

And as it was three years before, it is my mother who tells me. A week maybe more has passed and I cannot reach my father and this man who has called me daily, this man who has never missed a weekend, is suddenly a ghost. I make calls, my mother does too, and then one night she sits me down on her bed.

It's your father, she says. He is going back to prison.

And in the room where my mother once told me that I had a new father, the room where she has now told me I have lost my new father, I collapse. I know prison had been part of Gabriel's life, but it had not been part of the life we shared together. Our life together was about healing. I have no concept of my father this way, captured, in chains.

And my father, gone but still present, a space in my heart. I don't understand, I sob to my mother. She tells me it's true. She tells me my Grandma Vina is the one who confirmed it.

Mom had called and called in this age before the ubiquity of mobile phones and after three weeks, maybe four, she got Grandma Vina. And in these days, long before the influential determined that our criminal justice system needed reform, all we have is the shame of it, we who are families. There are no support groups, no places to discuss what is happening. I don't even learn—although I guess—that he is reincarcerated on a drug charge. But I don't ask. I don't know to ask.

It will be more than a decade before I meet the advocate and scholar Deborah Small, who will say that this is a nation founded on addiction—the production of rum and other alcohols, tobacco, sugar. And now, she will say, they put people in prison for it. Prison was not always the response to drug use, she will say to a me who is grown and able to process what became of a man I loved.

But when I am a girl, a teenager heading into my junior year in high school who is crying in my mother's bedroom, I only know one thing. If prisons are supposed to make society more safe, why do I feel so much fear and hurt?

In 1986 when I am three years old, Ronald Reagan reenergizes the drug war that was started in 1971 by Richard Nixon by further militarizing the police in our communities, which swells the number of Black and Latinx men who are incarcerated. Between 1982 and 2000, the number of people locked up in the state of California grows by 500 percent. And it will be nearly a quarter of a century before my home state is forced, under consent decree, to reduce the number of people it's locked up, signaling, we hope, the end of what will eventually be called the civil rights crisis of our time. A generation of human beings, Black women, Black children and Black men, including my father and eventually my brother, who are viewed as having no other meaningful role in our nation except as prisoners.

Prisoners are valuable. They not only work for pennies for the corporate brands our people love so much, but they also provide jobs for mostly poor white people, replacing the jobs lost in rural communities. Poor white people who are chosen to be guards. They run the motels in prison towns where families have to stay when they make 11-hour drives into rural corners of the state. They deliver the microwave food we have to buy from the prison vending machines.

And companies pay for the benefit of having prisoners,

legally designated by the Constitution as slaves, forced to do their bidding. Forget American factory workers. Prisoners are cheaper than even offshoring jobs to eight-year-old children in distant lands. License plates are being made in prisons along with 50 percent of all American flags, but the real money in this period of prison expansion in the 80s, 90s and early 2000s is made by Victoria's Secret, Whole Foods, AT&T and Starbucks. And these are just a few. Stock in private prisons and companies attached to prisons represents the largest growth industry in the American market as the millennium lurches toward its barbed-wire close.

There are no rulebooks to guide you through losing a parent to incarceration, although the year my father goes back, there are literally ten million children living in the United States who know this loss.

But there are no self-help books and there are no prayers.

Michelle Alexander has not yet written The New Jim Crow.

Barack Obama has not yet been elected and has not left office with the largest reduction in federal prisoners in history.

The racially discriminatory sentencing imbalance between crack and powder cocaine has not yet been addressed.

Hundreds of millions of dollars have not yet flowed into non-profits to fight mass incarceration.

Bill Keller has not left his high post at The New York Times *to assume leadership at the Marshall Project, and Justice Strategies has not created its blog for children of the incarcerated.*

Angela Davis has not yet asked us, Are Prisons Obsolete? *and Ruthie Gilmore has not yet done breathtaking research on prisons in California and beyond.*

But in the small world you occupy in El Barrio in Van Nuys, you do not know that there are millions of teenagers and children feeling what you are feeling, experiencing what you are experiencing, the disorientation, the loss of stability, of safety, the sure knowledge that you can wake up one morning and find anyone, maybe everyone, gone.

You only know what you can calculate:

He will miss your high school performances.

He will miss your graduation.

He will miss four birthday celebrations—your eighteenth!

There will be no more Thanksgivings at Grandma's, no Christmases.

The kisses and hugs that once embarrassed you and then sustained you will also be gone.

You do not have words to explain any of this, the full measure of the loss. Do words even exist to explain some forms of devastation, are there pictures that approximate in real-world terms what the shattered heart of a Black girl looks like?

This is why you tuck it away quietly in secret pockets.

This is why you act like you are fine.

This is why you go to school and pretend that algebraic equations that never add up to your father coming home make some kind of sense.

This is why sometimes you think, I can't breathe.

I can't breathe.

I can't breathe.

4

MAGNITUDE AND BOND

We are each other's harvest;
We are each other's business;
We are each other's magnitude and bond

GWENDOLYN BROOKS

Just as I am beginning to adjust to all the changes that becoming a Brignac brought on, I have to adjust to what it means to set them aside. My father's family loves me, but with only four years together, I am still not fully part of their everyday. Which is to say that with my father out of sight, so am I, and it will remain this way for all the years he is gone.

I do not see them.

We do not talk on the phone.

We are a part of each other's past; and looking ahead toward an unknowable future, it begins to dawn on me the full measure of the role that my father played in the family, the literally magnetic role.

Gabriel pulled us closer. He was the reason for our family to all come in from the rain. Together. With him gone, there are no more uncles playing baseball every weekend, my cousin Naomi tells me. We go, for a time, to the same high school, and she is the one who keeps me in the loop.

There are no more football Saturdays together.

There's no more poor man's gumbo eaten together over laughter and shouted conversations.

There are holidays, but without Gabriel's healing spirit to make the room easy, I can't imagine what those holidays are possibly like. And anyway, I am not invited.

Still I have come to love Gabriel and he loves me and we seek to stay connected.

I cannot go to see my father without an adult to take me and even if I could, I don't want to go alone. Gabriel and I stay in touch through letter writing. Our letters are brief. My father always opens his in the exact same way:

Dearest Patrisse,
I hope this letter finds you well . . .

In each letter he apologizes. He says he misses me. In each letter he promises us better, brighter times.

In my responses, I tell him I miss him, too. I say I cannot wait to see him again. But in the letters we do not speak of the prison itself, his experience inside, locked up and away. We do not talk about what he was convicted of, although I suspect it's drugs because drugs are what I know most people seem to be getting locked up for. But in those letters, those weekly notes, it's almost as though he could have been writing from a school or a country far, far away. Which is why I do not tell him about my life, either, the interior of it and in particular Monte, who, right behind my father, is also sent to prison.

There comes a day when I am at dance class and it is Monte's job to come and pick me up. He doesn't, but I don't panic. He has, by that time, started acting strangely. There was the day he burst into my room excited and full of love. This is for you, Trisse, he had said, and handed me a ten-dollar bill, all crisp and fresh. Before the night was over he returned, eyes desperate and pleading. Trisse, can I get that ten dollars back, he asked softly but insistently. Of course I gave it back, along with a piece of my spirit.

But my mother, whom I call on the day Monte doesn't come to get me, tells me to take the bus home, which I do, giving me time to think about my brother. I figured he was getting high, the cause of the wild mood swings, the hours spent locked in the bathroom when I'd hear him sobbing.

Monte, I'd say from one side of the door. Monte, let me in! I love you!

Go way Trisse, he'd sob, and then refuse to speak anymore.

Except when he did speak more. Because that was the other side of him. There were days and nights when my brother did not sleep, when he chattered on incessantly, was sure like no one has ever been sure before that he could grab this thing, this life, by the horns and go! I don't, we don't, know which Monte will greet us on any good morning, on any long night. And in many ways, we just go with it, I just go with it. We don't know what else to do and, besides, doesn't Monte have a right to his inconsistent space? He never knows how the world will greet him, after all.

I spent my childhood watching my brother get arrested. Once, when I was 12 we were just walking down the street, Monte and I, and a cop we saw regularly came up to us.

Are you Monte Cullors? he barked.

Yes, my brother responded.

And that was it. In front of me he handcuffed Monte and took him away. I had no idea what for. To this day I have no idea what for. All I know is that this was a common occurrence. And not just with Monte. It's hard for me to think of a boy in my neighborhood who didn't spend time in juvenile hall, or wasn't arrested at least once.

It is interesting to me now to think that at the time this was happening, a time when my mother worked multiple jobs that still barely amounted to a livable wage, a time when Alton had been closed out of the industry he'd given his life to and no replacement had been offered or created, and a time when Gabriel was given prison rather than treatment, Americans, Black and white, were deeply involved in the final push to end apartheid in South Africa. At his trial at Rivonia, Nelson Mandela would say the following in his famous "I Am Prepared to Die" speech:

*Our fight is against real, and not imaginary, hardships . . .
poverty and lack of human dignity. . . . The lack of human
dignity experienced by Africans is the direct result of the policy
of white supremacy. White supremacy implies black inferiority.
Legislation designed to preserve white supremacy entrenches
this notion. . . .*

*They do not look upon them as people with families of
their own; they do not realize that they have emotions—
that they fall in love like white people do; that they want to
be with their wives and children like white people want to be
with theirs; that they want to earn enough money to support
their families properly, to feed and clothe them and send
them to school.*

He continued,

*Poverty and the breakdown of family life have secondary ef-
fects. Children wander about the streets of the townships
because they have no schools to go to, or no money to enable
them to go to school, or no parents at home to see that they
go to school, because both parents (if there be two) have to
work to keep the family alive. This leads to . . . a growing
violence which erupts not only politically, but everywhere.
Life in the townships is dangerous. . . .*

*Africans want to be paid a living wage. Africans want
to perform work which they are capable of doing. . . . Africans want to be allowed to own land in places where they
work, and not to be obliged to live in rented houses which
they can never call their own. Africans want to be part of the*

general population, and not confined to living in their own
ghettoes. Africans want a just share in the whole of South
Africa; they want security and a stake in society. . . .
    Above all, we want equal political rights, because with-
out them our disabilities will be permanent.

In almost every way, Mandela speaking in 1964 at the
trial at Rivonia could have been one of our leaders speaking for Los Angeles in 1992, the year of the uprising. Mon-
ies were being spent unequally for schools. Our programs
were cut. Our parents had the most meager of jobs. Our
families were torn asunder. I begin to realize this when I am
provided a basis for comparison. Like the one I get when
I am still in middle school at Millikan.

There, I am close friends with Tiffany, a white girl who goes
there. She, like the other children, lives in Sherman Oaks
and there comes a day when she invites me home with her
for dinner. I go. And as the sun begins to set, we, the whole
family plus me, gather in a fully separate dining room and
the sweet, round man who is her father asks us about our
day, what we learned, what we cared about and dreamed of
for ourselves. Have you thought about what you want to be
when you grow up, Patrisse?

It is incredible. Who asks children such things and over
a well-set table where all the family has gathered to eat, converse? I've only seen that in movies, on the TV shows I
love, *90210*. But this is real life and here I am.

Have I ever known such a moment in my own home? My

mother is gone before 6:00 in the morning each day and home after 10:00 at night. This is our life. This has always been our life. And while we live and we love and we laugh, there is also an unmitigated and unmitigating arc of pain that is there, has always been there, just below the surface. We suspect that things are not supposed to be this way but we aren't sure what the other way is.

But in any case I am having dinner at my friend's home, at her table, with her parents and I will tell you now that the sweet, round man, the father who asked his daughter—and me!—about our day and our dreams, I will tell you that over a few visits and discussions about life and where I lived we, he and I, come to realize that we know each other, the father and I. Or, at least he knows my mother.

He is, this father, this gentle inquisitor of my days and my dreams, to put it frankly, our family's slum lord. He owns many buildings there in our Van Nuys hood, our poor hood. Our colored hood. Our building is one of the ones he owns. He is the very same man who allowed my family to subsist without a working refrigerator for the better part of a year. The coincidence is so shocking to me. I don't know what to say, so I say nothing. I think if I say something, someone would think I was making it up, eating a big meal with a friend whose sweet father doesn't care that my family has no way to do the same. I could understand someone thinking I was lying, embellishing, at the least, for dramatic effect.

But I wouldn't have been. And I'm not now.

It is as true as the fact that our Van Nuys neighborhood, bordering as it did the wealthy white neighborhood of Sherman Oaks, was ground zero for the war on drugs and the war on gangs. There could be no spillover of us, the others, the *dark* others. We, our poverty and our music and our different foods and our reminders that they, the residents of our pretty adjacent neighborhood, were wealthy only at our expense, could not seep into the neat white world of Sherman Oaks. Of course that's not what they said, that they didn't want to be reminded of what it took to keep themselves rich.

It was the 1990s and what was mostly said—in carefully chosen language—was that being born Black or Mexican was enough to label you a gang member, a dangerous drug-involved criminal. And there were few leaders, save for perhaps Maxine Waters, saying that it was all bullshit. A group of kids hanging out in the street—because there were no parks and rec, no programming, nothing except sidewalks and alleyways to hang out in—became a gang. And it was mostly boys rounded up in those years. Boys, the initial wide swath of collateral damage in the war on gangs, the war on drugs, both of these names code for *round up all the niggers you can.*

There was no education plan for us—school budgets had been decimated and a decade before Reagan had declared ketchup was a vegetable so that's what we were fed, we who counted on school breakfast and lunch to get through the day. With no education plan for us or thought about us becoming arbiters of our own destiny or self-determining contributors to an economy designed to reward only a few, the only plan left for us was prison or death.

If we did not die, we could go to prison, where we could work for the State of California and corporate brands we could not afford to buy. And the apprenticeship for this kind of work, the work that gets done in prisons, it started young. It started when Monte and his friends were way little. Little boys were cycled in and out of detention centers, places where they were trained and tracked, readied for longer stretches in prisons far away. They were often beaten and abused, regularly humiliated by having to strip, piss and shit publicly, left to discover their sexuality in the presence of people who hated them, and then they were sent back out to tell people they were hard, they were strong and they were a human testimony to other little boys: This is your future. Get ready. Man the fuck up.

And although I don't agree with this approach to public safety, I suppose it could be argued forcefully that the removal of one difficult person, the local thief or bully, perhaps, makes a community more safe.

But for us, for Black people, the mass incarceration of first our fathers and later our mothers made our lives entirely unsafe. There were almost no adults who were there, present to love and nurture and defend and protect us. There was almost no one to say our dreams and our lives and our hopes mattered. And so we did it ourselves, the best way we knew how.

This, more than anything, was the evolution of gangs in Van Nuys. The groups of kids they first called gangs were really young people who were friends, they were my friends, and they took a defensive posture against what looked and felt like an actual advancing army that came in on foot and came in police cars for which the county had appropriated ever more dollars to patrol us with. And worse than the cars, most frightening of all, were the helicopters overhead. At all hours of day and night they hovered above us, shone lights into the midnight, circling and surveilling, vultures looking for the best next prey.

And there was Monte. My Monte. My brother.

He and his friends—really all of us—were out there trying to stay safe against the onslaught of adults who, Vietnamlike, saw the enemy as anyone Black or Brown who moved. He and his friends were not only busted but sent away for:

1. Tagging
2. Underage drinking
3. Carrying two-inch pocket knives
4. Cutting class
5. Being kids
6. Talking shit
7. Talking back
8. Wearing the same t-shirts. Literally.

And the gang statutes were written so broadly that even members of Congress, under their definition, could have been arrested. The ACLU would document that,

Gang injunctions make otherwise legal, everyday activities—such as riding the bus with a friend or picking a spouse up from work late at night—illegal for people they target.

They further argued, rightly, that,

One of the most troubling aspects is that they often give police overly-broad discretion to label people gang members without having to present any evidence or even charge someone with a crime. Police are left to rely on things like what someone looks like, where they live, and who they know. As a result, there is a great potential for racial profiling, with a particular impact on young people of color. Despite the documented existence of white gangs, no California gang injunction has targeted a white gang.

Kids were being sent away simply for being alive in a place where war had been declared against us. And the propaganda, the rationalizing of how much we needed to be destroyed, we the generation called super-predators, was promoted by people who were Republican and Democrat, and, save for a few, Black as well as white. It was such convenient reasoning: the hoisting of responsibility on the narrow, non-voting shoulders (and after too many busts, never-voting shoulders) of 13 year olds, 14, 15 and 16 year olds, thereby absolving grown people of any responsibility themselves. As soon as you said drugs, as soon as you said gangs, you didn't have to talk about what it meant to throw a bunch of adolescents together in a community with no resources, no outlets, no art classes, no mentorship, no love but from their families who were being harmed, cut daily, themselves.

And it didn't matter how poorly conceived and executed the gang statutes were, what with their siphoning off of millions and millions and millions of dollars into police departments and away from everything that any rational parent or adult knows a young person needs in order to succeed— good schools, creative outlets, arts and sports programs and space to just be still. But so ineffective were these laws that between 1990 and 2010 in my city, Los Angeles, with the greatest number of injunctions in the state designed, they said, to stop gang activity, 10,000 young people were killed. Which is why with no one else on our side, we sided with ourselves. For better and for motherfucking worse.

A friend asked me once, well what about Paul? How come he wasn't swept up and sent away? Paul, I explain, my brother, was never a child, I say. Once Alton was gone, it was Paul who made us breakfast and dinner and got us into bed. Paul, the man of the house before he was even a teenager in the house. Paul was never a child, doing things that children do: hanging out, being loud in the street, engaging in silly, risky behavior that is the hallmark of becoming an adult. Paul was 40 before he was 14. That's what about Paul, I say.

Even still, when Monte is arrested and faces a charge of attempted robbery, which means real prison time, a new terror sets in. We know about juvenile hall—juvie—how to navigate it, but this is wholly different. At just 19 years old, Monte is in jail for two long months before we can even locate him. My mother calls and calls and tries and tries but the bars on the outside are as thick and real as the bars on the inside. Finally there is a breakthrough—after multiple visits someone allows my mother to see my brother. Why then, who knows? Jail and prison rules are capricious no matter what is said on paper. And alone, my mother goes to see her child in Twin Towers Detention Center, one of the many jails that makes up the Los Angeles County jail system.

It will be years, I will be grown, before she tells me what she saw, the child she bore, the one who loved animals and who once laughed easily, her big six-foot-two son, emaciated, more than 40 pounds gone from his suddenly frail frame. He is bruised and beaten. By who? My mother demands to know, but Monte won't say. He is too scared to say. Years will pass before I learn that Monte was in a full-blown episode when he was taken to jail. He was hearing voices. His mind had been folded in on itself, and shaken brutally. The jail psychiatrist is the first to provide a diagnosis that explains why Monte has these mood swings, this erratic behavior: he has schizoaffective disorder. But they do not tell us this.

We learn it later, much later. After he is in prison. Way after. Like we will learn later that the sheriffs at the LA County

Jail were the ones who beat him for his illness. They beat him and they kept water from him and they tied him down, four-point hold, and they drugged him nearly out of existence. There are drugs to take when a person is having a psychotic break. Those drugs can bring the person back into a good or total semblance of themselves. This was not what they did to my brother. They drugged Monte to incapacitate him, to in-capacitate his humanity. To leave him with no dignity.

On the day my mother finds Monte and visits him in the LA County Jail through the glass that separates mother and son, he is barely able to hold himself up.

He is drooling on himself.

He is unable to speak a single full sentence coherently.

But he is able to raise his hand to the glass, where my mother, shaking, meets it on the other side.

I love you, my child, my baby, my son. I love you so much.

Monte is charged with attempted burglary after he is caught trying to sneak into someone's home through a window. He is looking at six years in prison. He explains to our mother in one of their phone calls what happened was beyond his control.

They told me to do it, he confesses to her. They made me, he whispers through the phone lines. *They* being an en-tity only he can see or hear.

In the prison he is sent to, Monte lives out his sentence in the mental health unit. Almost immediately upon his ar-rival, he is stabbed by a member of a Mexican gang. My Black brother who had grown up around Mexicans and sought to identify with them behind the wall, finds that in prison the lines are different. Blacks are only allowed to stay with Blacks. Mexicans with Mexicans. Whites with whites. Even young white boys who go to prison—they are forced to join Aryan gangs no matter what they really believe. It is how you stay alive.

Or else go to the mental health unit. Which is what Monte does. I am safe here, he tells my mother, who tells me. Although a mental health unit in a prison is hardly what I would come up with when I think of keeping someone safe, he is probably right and it's also true he is never stabbed again.

There are more people with mental health disorders in prison than in all of the psychiatric hospitals in the United States added up. In 2015, the *Washington Post* reported that,

> American prisons and jails housed an estimated 356,268 [people] with severe mental illness. . . . [a] figure [that] is more than 10 times the number of mentally ill patients in state psychiatric hospitals [in 2012, the last year for reliable data]—about 35,000 people.

Monte writes me letters almost every week, none of which are coherent and all of which are dark. He talks a lot about crying, and totally unbidden and untethered he often writes JEHOVAH in all caps. And sometimes, sometimes he writes, WE WILL BE FREE!

I am 16. My brother is in prison. My new father is in prison. There are no support services for teens with family in prison. There are no school counselors to speak to who can help me understand all that I am feeling. But there are friends and I pull them close and I pull them tight.

There's Rosa, who becomes my first friend when I enter the ninth grade at Cleveland High School, where none of my middle school or neighborhood friends attend. Cleveland is a charter school centered on social justice and the arts, but I am still nervous not knowing anyone. Rosa changes that. She's dark-skinned and Mexican and gentle with me when I need it the most. She introduces herself to me right off and says, I like your Bob Marley t-shirt! And with that, we are bonded. In the mornings we share breakfasts she brings from home.

In the afternoons and evenings we write in a best friend journal that we pass back and forth. We rock like this through ninth grade and then through tenth and in eleventh grade we expand our friendship to include Carla, whom I meet through another person I've become close to, Cheyenne. Cheyenne and I will become just about as close as two people can get, but I am still drawn to Carla, who is loud in the hallways and obnoxious in a way that is exciting and she's Queer. She's bold in presenting all of who she is and for this she becomes my shero. Like she is to this very day.

But it is these sisters I turn to, first in the pages of the best friend journal, when I can no longer hold in what is happening to my brother. And one day I ask them—Rosa and

Carla—would you write to him, too? And they agree. In some ways, Monte becomes their brother, too.

Unlike in the letters he's written to me, when Monte writes back to Rosa and Carla he is coherent. I don't understand then because I don't know yet about his diagnosis and how to read when he's properly medicated, when he is not. I am just grateful I have these young women beside me. This family we are creating.

In 2003, two years after I graduate high school, Monte is released from prison. And it is Carla who has a car and who will be the one who drives me to pick him up from the Greyhound bus station. The prison loaded him onto a bus on one side of the state and now, finally, here he is disembarking on our side. I am excited beyond the telling and then I see him, for the first time since he was taken in 1999. But when I see him, I am left breathless.

My brother is hunched over. He is swollen from all the medication he's on. He descends the bus steps in the clothes the prison gave him to return to us in: a thin muscle shirt and a pair of boxer shorts. They gave him underwear, but no pants, their final fuck you, you ain't human to this man whom I have loved for all of my life. If we had not been there to scoop him right up, I'm sure Monte would have been picked up and sent back to some jail.

Monte with shower shoes on his feet, Locs sunglasses on his face like a celluloid gangsta. Monte carries with him a single manila envelope with his discharge papers inside and the medication they sent him home with. He has crushed all the pills. It is clear that the prison "doctors" chose not to stabilize Monte before he boarded the bus. Indeed, my brother is in the throes of a full-blown episode.

Not that I fully understand this yet.

I just know he is here, he is with me, he is free. I gather myself and then, Monte! I squeal. I try to hug him, but he hops in the front seat of Carla's car and is silent.

How are you? I push.

Okay, comes the reply, hard and fast.

I missed you so much, I say.

Okay, he says.

We arrive at our home where the family is waiting, and a Welcome Home Monte party is about to be in full effect. Paul has a video camera out and our nephew, Chase, the child Monte had before he was sent away, is trying to jump on a father he has never had a chance to know. Monte heads to our table and sits there like a zombie and from the corner of my eye, I see it, the pain in the face of my so strong mother. She looks as if she will break, but she does not break.

He's here, Mom. It's okay. He's here, I say.

And we hold on to that, to this small offering, over the next few days as Monte doesn't sleep, doesn't eat but rubs toothpaste on walls and mixes drinks with pieces of tissue or else runs outside and screams, I'm walking the line! I'm walking the line! He takes to wearing two pairs of shoes. He slips on one first, and then over the first pair, he slips on another.

By day four, Monte brings a shopping cart filled with God knows what into the living room, and for some reason, this is what does it, what breaks my mother. Her tears rush forward hard, the destroyed levees of Lake Pontchartrain. We are holed up in the bedroom, locking ourselves away. We are confused and afraid and my mother is crying. I have never seen her cry before.

Monte is growing ever more erratic. When he speaks he babbles and nothing we say is able to get through to him. We have no idea what to do as my brother spirals and spirals. Jasmine has left, gone to stay with a friend. She's the youngest and completely overwhelmed.

I call a friend, a former teacher, Vitaly, who is a therapist and describe what is happening. This is what an episode looks like, he tells me. I try to coax Monte but he won't talk to me. And then success! Eventually he does talk to Bernard, the man my mother will fall in love with after Alton and marry. We—well, Bernard—are trying to convince Monte it's time to go to the hospital. Monte seems to be listening to this man who is a stranger to him and we guess he has grown accustomed to only speaking with men. I call an ambulance and do a mini-intake over the phone but they will not come to help when they hear his background.

He is a felon, they say. You have to call the police.

I beg. Please help us. This isn't a criminal matter.

They refuse. They disconnect the line. My mother and I go back and forth and decide we have no other choice. I call the local law enforcement office and explain everything.

I beg them to go slow. I tell them Monte's history with police because by now I know how he was beaten and tortured by LA County sheriffs.

Two rookies arrive and they are young as fuck. I meet them downstairs. I ask them, What will you do if my brother gets violent?

Monte's never been violent but I am trying to prepare for anything. I'm—we're—in a place we've never been.

We'll just taser him, one responds.

No! My God! Absolutely not!

I refuse to let them past me until they promise me they won't hurt him, and when they finally do, I lead them into the apartment, explaining to Monte as I walk through the door, It's okay. It's okay. They're just here to help.

And my brother. My big, loving, unwell, good-hearted brother, my brother who has rescued small animals and my brother who has never, never hurt another human being, drops to his knees and begins to cry. His hands are in the air. He is sobbing.

Please don't take me back. Please don't take me back.

I stop cold. I tell the police they have to leave and they do and I get down on the floor. I curl up next to Monte. I hold him as much as he'll allow.

I am so sorry, Monte, I say, my voice broken, my face wet with tears. I am so, so, sorry.

Eventually, Bernard nudges him gently and gets him to agree to a walk. They go to the supermarket, where apparently Monte knocks everything down. They go to the movies and Monte tries to tear up the seats. And finally, finally, Bernard gets Monte to agree to come with him to the hospital, which is where he stays for almost three weeks. It takes two weeks alone just to get him stabilized on the right medication before we, his family, are allowed to go visit him.

When people ask me how we got through that moment, that time, how we managed it all, I tell them about my mother, Cherice. I tell them about a woman who worked from can't see in the morning until can't see at night. I tell them about a woman whose own family had disavowed her but who refused to be a person who disavowed anyone in return. My mother wove us together, my brothers, sister and I, into a tight and strong complex quilt and she called it us and it was, and it is, us.

Magnitude and Bond.

5

WITNESS

The paradox of education is precisely this—that as one be-gins to become conscious one begins to examine the society in which he is being educated.

JAMES A. BALDWIN

Zora Neale Hurston once wrote that there are years that ask questions and years that answer them. In my own life, my high school years did both and all at once and con-sistently. My new magnet program, Cleveland High, is lo-cated in Reseda, another San Fernando Valley neighborhood not so different from my own Van Nuys hood, though a half-step more developed. Reseda is all strip malls and fast-food joints and is mostly Latinx and working class. None of my friends from middle school are sent there so in every way it is an ending as much as it is a beginning.

Cleveland's humanities program is rooted in social justice and we study apartheid and communism in China. We study Emma Goldman and read bell hooks, Audre Lorde. We unpack the world's three major religions—and are allowed to go deeper into lesser-known and practiced religions if that's where our inquiries take us. We are encouraged to challenge racism, sexism, classism and heteronormativity. We are encouraged to ask, How do you know what you think you know?

It is inevitable, then, that I begin to question the Jehovah's Witness world I had come up in. It begins with small questions posed to the Elders, the group of men only who guide Kingdom Hall, our understanding of the Bible, our way of worship.

There are things I need to know and so I begin to ask:

How can we preach that the Earth is only 2,000 years old?

How come only 144,000 people are chosen to go to heaven? What happens to the rest and how is the selection made? Wouldn't heaven be lonely with only 144,000 people?

Why is there no mention of dinosaurs in the Bible? (I am obsessed with dinosaurs at the time.) Do Jehovah's Witnesses believe in dinosaurs? (The answer—yes—is one of the few clear ones I receive.)

And then my inquiries push further: Why are all the Elders in our religion men?

What about the women?

And why would a religion encourage family members not to speak to one another?

This is when I begin to hear that Satan has gotten me,

but those words, those admonishments, don't change the reality within which I have lived for the whole of my life, the life of an exiled family, a family cast off of the precious island that is Kingdom Hall.

When my mother was a teenager and pregnant, she was immediately disassociated from the religion—and from her family. The religion took precedence over the love and support she must have needed from her mother, her father. Thrown out of her home, she was not even allowed to speak to her parents or siblings. The religion was more important than a scared 16 year old or us, her children, who were often hungry and often without but were not allowed to ask our own family for help. My mother's family was not rich, but neither were they wanting. We were allowed the privilege to come and to pray but not to participate in fellowship or even say hello to other members of Kingdom Hall, except the Elders, no matter the relationship.

And for years, for the whole of my early childhood years and into my early teens, my mother worked and worked and tried and tried and kept showing up to prove to the Elders that she was reformed, a good and pious woman. When I am in the ninth grade she writes them a letter asking to be reinstated. She speaks in the letter about why she is worthy. And after some deliberation by the men, and after two decades of being disassociated, they tell my mother her arguments are meritorious, which is to say she will be reinstated. It will be a public affair.

And I suppose that I should be happy for this development. But now, after all of these years of being a Disassociated Witness, of being allowed to go to the Kingdom Hall but not allowed to speak to anyone, including my mother's family—You can come and pray but you are too dirty, and by extension your children are too dirty, to speak with, even if you share the same blood—now, after all these years, I feel something like disgust, certainly something like anger.

For four years I have watched my father in faith-based processes where he could own his choices and still be embraced, still be loved. And that practice, that coming together, that speaking the truth of your life from a place beyond shame and having it heard from a place beyond judgment, it didn't just change my father. It changed we who were witnesses. It changed me who was a witness.

And a thought occurs to me after my mother is reinstated. When was she ever given such grace? Was she ever given such grace? Had she ever lived and been free in even the smallest corner of the world where she was not judged and shamed? Was this the place that could offer her or any one of us this?

I am only 14, and while there is a lot I know I don't know, there are some things I do.

I want a place of worship that feels honest. Kingdom Hall, with its men over everyone and literal interpretation of the Bible, does not feel honest. I cannot look in the face of those judging men and believe that they truly are the ones who could hold my mother to account. I do not believe that in all of time, only 144,000 people would survive and not be cast into a Lake of Fire.

I want mentorship and guidance, not this judgment and

punishment I had known all my life. It feels particularly aimed at women and our bodies, our sexuality. My mother was spiritually exiled for choosing to love someone when she was a teenager and, as evidence of that love, birthing beautiful children—and with a man, Alton, who would choose me, too. Twenty years she carried the heavy water for that love. Twenty years!

I know I am supposed to be on a spiritual path, but the path that Jehovah's Witness has me on does not feel liberating or purposeful—beyond the purpose of shaming and scaring us. It doesn't provide me the feeling of connection and spirit I feel reading Audre Lorde, whose books I carry with me everywhere. Where I can find no center for myself in the Bible, what with its anti-woman origin story, I can when I read the essays in Audre's *Sister Outsider*. I am changing, my whole life is changing, and for all the parts that feel terrifying and hard, there are other parts, many of them, that feel incredibly exciting and bursting with possibility. The possibility of becoming my truest self.

On the day of the reinstatement, my mother is nonchalant. We are readying ourselves to go to Kingdom Hall in the same way we always do. Eat a light breakfast. Talk little. Dress conservatively. On that morning, in fact, we do not even know what is about to happen. Now I realize my mother's way of coping is to minimize things, both the good and the bad, but especially the bad. It's how she manages trauma. But on that day we enter Kingdom Hall, as always, silently, because here is a place where you do not speak, not even whisper.

My mother takes out a piece of paper and a pen and scribbles a note that she passes to us, her children: I'm getting reinstated today, she writes. And as they begin the public portion of the service, I start to feel sick. Not physically but emotionally. It is insulting! How dare they! After all we'd gone through, after the years of hunger and uncertainty and their lack of support—and after all that my mother had done to provide for us, who the hell are they to judge this woman, my mother?

I get up from my seat and sit the service out in a bathroom stall. I will not bear witness to this vulgar hypocrisy. This body of men judging the body and very soul of my hardworking and underpaid mother. In that hour and in that place, being a Jehovah's Witness becomes something that exists as part of my past. And beyond the doors of the Kingdom Hall, I set out to find God, to find my spirit, to find myself.

6

OUT IN THE WORLD

*I remember how being young and Black and gay and lonely
felt. A lot of it was fine, feeling I had the truth and the
light and the key, but a lot of it was purely hell.*

AUDRE LORDE

I always knew I wasn't heterosexual. Which is not
to say I focused on that as a child. It wasn't much of an issue
then and, like my friends, I also acted boy-crazy. But I never
felt it in my soul. The one boyfriend I had in middle school
would end up coming out as Gay when he got older.

I was a girl who had come of age in a repressive sexual
environment. In Kingdom Hall we would spend hours and
hours being instructed on sinful sexual behavior, which included lectures on masturbation. Not masturbating was elevated to a moral position, which is to say normal, healthy

sexual expression was considered immoral. In many ways, it was my high school, Cleveland, that saved my life.

And while Cleveland was nowhere near perfect, it offered a pathway for we who were Queer to claim ourselves. Nevertheless, while Ellen DeGeneres had come out on live TV, in our own lives, there were no Gay Straight Alliances, no LGBTQ groups, no counselors trained to guide us through our particular struggles, which often included being kicked out of our homes.

There was one student group called Impact that had really been organized for kids struggling with depression, but many LGBTQ kids ended up in there because depression is the predictable outcome when people are forced to deny their humanity. Along my own path, I had a particular and magnificent guide, a North Star. Her name was Naomi. She was my cousin and touchstone.

Naomi was why, in some ways, while I came into Cleveland alone and without my middle school friends, in other ways, it was like coming home. Both a public and a humanities magnet institution, it served as the local school for many of my cousins on my father's side of the family. Most of them were boys and on the sports teams and I didn't interact with them very much. But Naomi was the daughter of my father's cousin James who, like Gabriel, had come to LA from Eunice, Louisiana, at the age of nine. Gabriel and James grew up as best friends: two country mice trying to make their way among some big old city mice. Naomi and I were shaping up to mirror the love of our fathers. She held me close, even at one of the hardest moments in her own life.

We, Naomi and I, started the ninth grade together. Everyone seemed to know and love her. They'd all gone to middle school together but that wasn't the only thing. Naomi was—is—outgoing and beautiful. She was a star on the track team and could kick it with anyone, the roughest wanna-be gangstas and the Emo white girls. And of course, us, we, the Black girls, loved her, though none more than me. On top of it all, Naomi did something several of us wished we had the courage to do: she came right out, bold as love, and had a gorgeous girlfriend who was *older*.

And even though in our family, on my father's side that is, there was pretty broad acceptance of Queer people— we had aunties who openly identified as Gay—Naomi, who was masculine of center, what we called then a Stud, did not have a mother who was one of those people. Cousin James had married a woman who was deeply homophobic, and when Naomi comes out, it sends her over the edge into full-on abuse.

Marsha, Naomi's mother, explodes when she learns that her daughter has come out. And early one spring morning during our ninth-grade year when Naomi is at track practice with her coach and the other runners, Marsha bursts upon the scene. I am not there but quickly hear what happens; it rushes through the rest of the school like a California brush fire. Marsha grabs her daughter right there on the track and attacks her, fists and feet, beating her daughter down in front of all of her friends and coach until they are able to pull her

off. Then she screams at Naomi's coach that it is all her fault,
that she must have molested her daughter. And she makes a
threat: Naomi is going to be snatched out of Cleveland,
friendships, community, all be damned.

When friends find me and tell me I run through the
school to find my cousin, who is in a stairway crying. Crying because that's what Naomi does when she is angry. She
says the people at Cleveland are her family, her tribe. She
cannot lose us, she says.

I tell her we won't let go.

I tell her she is the heart of Cleveland.

We vow, through tears, to stay together.

And we do. Through the end of the semester and through
summer school. But when the fall rolls in, Naomi's mother
is true to her word. Naomi is enrolled in another school, in
another town. She is separated from her friends, loses her
coach, and is exiled from the community that had loved and
supported her since she was ten years old. And we who love
Naomi, we who love her and are Queer, whether we are out
or not, will learn in the harshest of ways that this is what it
means to be young and Queer: You can do nothing wrong
whatsoever, you can just be alive and yourself, and that is
enough to have the whole of your life smashed to the ground
and swept away. And all you can do is watch.

There are 20 girls of color who come out during my time
at Cleveland. I am one of them. In some ways I suppose
many of us are attracted to Cleveland because it is a social
justice school. It is artsy. And Columbine hasn't happened

yet so we don't yet have the bars and the metal detectors. Because that's what happened in the wake of the horrific school shooting in a town that was mostly white in a school that was mostly white. Black and Brown kids across the country got police in their schools, complete with drug-sniffing dogs, bars on the windows and metal detectors. Years on, as a member of the Los Angeles–based organization the Strategy Center, I will work on a campaign to end what is now known as the school-to-prison pipeline. This real-world horror for young Black and Brown people is summed up by the organization States of Incarceration, which reports that,

> In the quest to create "safe schools," students have become demoralized and criminalized. The presence of metal detectors, surveillance cameras, drug-sniffing dogs, harsh ticketing policies, and prison-inspired architecture has created a generation of students, usually poor and of color, who are always under surveillance and always under suspicion. These modes of controlling spaces and the youth within them normalize expectations of criminality, often fulfilled when everyday violations of school rules lead to ticketing, suspension, or worse, court summons and eventual incarceration—a direct path into the criminal justice system. . . . [Indeed], some school buildings become indistinguishable from prisons, police presence in them has continued to increase, with an

unequal impact on lower income schools with predominantly black and Latino student populations.
The Los Angeles Unified School District is one of
the districts nationwide to have its own police department, which has an annual budget of over $52
million specifically dedicated to its schools.

White campuses remain open air and green. But then
Cleveland is still fairly open and by the time I graduate a Gay
Straight Alliance has been formed.

One afternoon when I am in tenth grade, I go over to
Naomi's house so we can hang out for the afternoon. And I
look my cousin in the face and I say to my cousin, You know
Naomi, I am Bi. Bi is the terminology we use then.

She looks shocked and then scared. Is this the face she
wore the morning her mother, unhinged and hateful, had
come charging at her?

Then Naomi demands a re-hearing: What? What?

A pause, and then, We can't *both* be, she declares, she
almost screams. And yet we are. And I see it in her eyes,
the fear a person has for someone they love. The police hate
us. Schools don't really give a fuck about us. Don't be about
this life where even family can tell you to go to hell.

Moments pass. They are awkward. I have no idea what
to say so I return to what I do know: love.

I tell her about the five-foot-nine beauty out of the Le
Merk park area whose name is Cheyenne. She plays basketball and always carries a basketball, I say. We talk about

crystals and spirituality and we go to Barnes and Noble, I say. I tell her how we are reading books on race and gender and class. I tell her how we, Cheyenne and I, share poetry and that Cheyenne is a gifted writer. I tell her about Cheyenne's two little Afro-puffs. I tell her I love Cheyenne, that I am her world, that she is my world.

We talk for a long time, I don't remember everything we say. What I remember is that when I leave, Naomi understands. I remember that Naomi wants nothing more for me than my joy—and safety—and part of knowing safety in a world bristling with hate is to create these protected centers of love. I feel powerful. I feel strong.

Without hesitation, I start bringing Cheyenne home to hang out with me and we act oblivious to the awkwardness that permeates the small space we now occupy. I no longer have my own room because we no longer have our own apartment. Months before we had been evicted from the condo my mother had rented. She'd moved us into a new neighborhood in order to give us a better life and out of nowhere the owners wanted it back so they could sell it, which meant we had to just get the fuck out. We had 30 days' notice. A mother and three children tossed out like the trash. We were not trash. We were human beings.

It's Bernard, to whom my mother is engaged at the time, who comes to our rescue. He says, Don't worry, Cherice, I got you and your kids. Bernard moves us into his mother's one-bedroom apartment. His mother, a diabetic and wheelchair-bound elder, sleeps in the bedroom.

We take up residence in the living room, me and Jas-

mine, Mom and Bernard. Paul has moved out by now and
Monte is in prison. We sleep in sleeping bags on the floor.
Not an ideal situation in which to grow teens, one of whom
is Queer and whose father is in jail, but there we are. And
whenever possible, I invite Cheyenne over. I want some kind
of normalcy. Isn't this what teens are supposed to do? Hang
out in their houses with their girlfriends?

We, Cheyenne and I, feel the world can go to hell. We
love each other.

But it isn't easy. Beyond our few protected spaces—at
Cleveland there is a classroom, E-10, where the Queer kids
have taken up residence and made it our own and safe—the
streets are spilling with vitriol. Even with all of the hatred
that still exists today, it's amazing to think of the movement that has been made in the last 15 years.

But at the turn of the century it is all Fuck you, faggot!
and eyes filled with violence and disgust that follow us, that
train themselves on us. But we stay together, even when
Cheyenne drops out of school, as she eventually does. She
lives far from Cleveland High School and has little support
from her family when it comes to making it through high
school. She has no advocates, no one to ensure she gets
meals, let alone does her homework, or to navigate situations with teachers. And our schools are not set up to be
surrogates for the poorest of children, which is to say Cheyenne, which is to say most of us.

All of us need more than we are given or could possibly
access. Hell, our parents need more than they are given or
could access. Naomi eventually moves in with her father,

which alleviates much of the harm she lived with. Cousin
James is gentle and accepting and his love helps quell the
depression that has settled deeply inside her. Depression
rates run high among those of us who are out, and for those
of us rejected by our families, the national statistics report
we are 8.4 times as likely to attempt suicide. It is not a time
when Love is Love is Love is Love is a movement coming in
to rescue us.

For this reason, and much like the boys in my hood who
are the targets of police hatred and violence, we seek to create our own rescue plans, an effort that takes on a particular
significance when Carla is kicked out of her home in our
eleventh-grade year.

By the time this happens, and although I am still with
Cheyenne and Carla is still her homegirl, Carla and I have
developed a deep friendship of our own. We are thick as
thieves, besties for real, just as we are to this day. We decide that the only thing left to do is thug it out together. I
don't want to keep living with five people in the living room
of the apartment of a woman I barely know, feeling the judgment and silence that comes with being Queer in a Jehovah's Witness home where even masturbation is considered
deviant and where I have no space to say, Excuse me. I really
miss my father and my brother.

Carla and I begin to stay at the homes of different friends
as often as possible, and when it's not, we take to sleeping
in her car. By senior year, both of us are completely on our
own, couch surfing, going from friend's home to friend's
home to car to friend's home. I carry a duffel bag of clothes

and other personal-care items with me wherever I go. But when we graduate we get a reprieve in the form of our art history teacher, Donna Hill, with whom we are both close.

She tells us we can live with her while we get ourselves stabilized. I'm sure she thought it would take months, but I live there almost two years, and Carla almost three. We both work: me at Rite Aid, later as a dance teacher. But Donna neither charges us rent nor demands money for the food we eat that she buys. We act thoughtlessly, having friends over for small parties. We are kids and behave as such. Donna never yells at us, but she writes super-long letters about what our transgressions have been, what it means to live in community and be considerate.

She teaches us Transcendental Meditation—and an abiding patience with young people who are still evolving. Donna Hill, a simple, single Black woman with a heart that could carry a universe, becomes my first spirit guide, the first and most clear example I have as a young adult of what it means to receive a gift you can only properly show gratitude for by sharing it with others.

She is the first adult who doesn't think who we are, how we live and love, needs anything but support, some architecture. She understands our, Carla's and mine, emerging idea of building intentional family, a concept that I suppose will later become the basis of our theory of change.

To outsiders—in many cases outsiders being our families—our relationships may have seemed complex or odd or even dangerous. But to us they made sense. To us they were oxygen and still are. And although Cheyenne and I eventually separated and could not remain in touch, the rest of us remain close to this day, growing in numbers and love as the years roll on. And central to that growth, and complicating what I thought I knew about relationships and love, was a man named Mark Anthony, a brother who would become my first husband.

I didn't understand either when it first began.

I had never in my life been attracted to a heterosexual, cisgender man. There was, of course, Mikie in middle school, who was really Gay, but here I was almost grown with a man who was not Gay or Trans or Queer. I mean, what the hell?

Mark Anthony is a year younger than me, than my crew, and I meet him when I am a senior at Cleveland. I am a TA in his eleventh-grade cohort, and when I walk into the classroom, I cannot help but notice him. He is super attractive: tall and fair-skinned and with the greenest eyes I've ever seen.

I am totally confused by whatever happens immediately inside of me. I try to push it away, but Mark Anthony takes the bus with me one afternoon after we first meet and we talk about poetry and literature and music; he is the son of one of the original members of Earth, Wind & Fire. He watches me as I write in my journal on the bus that day and he tells me that he journals, too, and now I'm really getting invested but also really confused.

Am I really sitting here feeling attracted to some heterosexual dude?

But the energy between us is a tangible force. We, and not just us but anyone in our presence, can hold it in our hands. Even still and for the next few years we will channel it into a profoundly deep friendship. But we know it will be more. For a photography project Mark Anthony does with Donna about his journey, evolution and masculinity, he asks me for help. I take image after image of him but Carla shoots the last one of us. Our fists are in the air and we are holding hands looking out an open door, looking out toward a destiny that is not fully in view.

7

ALL THE BONES WE COULD FIND

We collected all the bones we could find, and yesterday, Natividad wrapped them in a shawl that she had knitted years ago. It was the most beautiful thing she owned.

"A thing like that should serve the living," Bankole said when she offered it.

"You are living," Natividad said.

OCTAVIA BUTLER, *PARABLE OF THE SOWER*

Gabriel comes home.

I am 20 years old and four years an organizer. My toe in the water around community organizing began while I was in high school but after I graduate I wade all the way in.

After graduation, Donna Hill not only provides a home for me, but also an outlet for all that I had learned in high school. She tells me about the Brotherhood Sisterhood social justice camp and for seven days I go off to the Pine Ridge campsite. There, we use icebreakers and experiential in-teractives to learn about not only systems of oppression, but more, how to be in courageous and compassionate relation-ships with people—all people. Campers are like me: poor, Queer and Black.

But they are also heterosexual. They are working and middle class and some are quite wealthy. They are Latinx. They are white. The goal is to train a generation to be in conversation with one another and we confront all manner of difference and all manner of discrimination. We talk about our families of origin and families of creation. We talk about racism, classism, sexism and heterosexism. We have highly facilitated, cross-racial dialogues that allow us to be wholly honest about the stereotypes we hold about one another.

One afternoon I listen to a young man speak in the group of 30 young people who identify as Queer. We are speaking about homophobia and the specific pain it causes, the deep depression it's wrought. We talk about what it's meant for so many of us to have been forced out of our homes by our par-ents. We talk about the rampant homelessness among us, the hunger, the isolation. And then this young brother says he doesn't expect he has long to live. He tells us he is 18 and has been diagnosed HIV positive and with that there is a grief in the room that cannot be contained. We grieve for him and we grieve because if we weren't aware of it before, now we cannot turn away: we live in a world where hatred is so deep that adults are fine ensuring death sentences for us young people who have done nothing but be in the world who we were born to be.

We resolve to fight back.

One of the organizations that comes to present to us while we are there is called the Strategy Center and I am immediately drawn to them and especially to their lead organizer, Kikanza Ramsey, whom I watch in a video. A sister with natural hair who is as fluid in Spanish as she is in English, I think: I want to be like her. I want to challenge structural inequities. I want to build power. In this space, we grow. I grow. I transform. After camp ends, I join the Strategy Center and for a year they train me to be an organizer.

I read, I study, adding Mao, Marx and Lenin to my knowledge of hooks, Lorde and Walker. I focus on young people and produce spoken-word events. I canvass as part of their Bus Riders' Union, a campaign that pushes back not only on climate change by highlighting the need to reduce reliance on cars, but also provides a workable and fair public transit system for people, like my mother, who rely on buses to get to work.

I meet and build with Eric Mann, who started the Strategy Center and who takes me under his wing. Eric is older and white and fearlessly anti-racist. He is also a man who worked the line at the GM plant just like Alton did. I find a home at the Strategy Center, a place that will raise me and hold me for more than a decade. I not only bring my friends to the Strategy Center, but also my father, who begins coming to meetings with me now that he is home from prison.

But it's not just Gabriel who becomes involved with me at the Strategy Center. His involvement slowly brings my mother around. My mother, who never had the luxury of time to attend meetings or participate in activities that could have made her life better. The Strategy Center will provide a place where, for the first time in the whole of my life, I will be in a public space with both of my parents—the way I had always seen my white friends in public spaces with both of their parents.

At their annual gala, The Political Party, after the videos and speeches—including my own—and after the drums and chants, we turn the joint into a huge dance party. And as my father and I dance the night away, my mother sits at our table at a fancy seat in the front. She watches us and smiles. My mother is a smiler. But she is not a dancer and never has been. Later she will say to me, This night took me back to when we were young, your father and I, and I used to go to the club with him. I didn't dance then either. He was always the dancer. But watching him move always made me so happy. Just like tonight.

After the struggles my mom and I had during high school, when Monte comes home I move back in with her to support my brother's caretaking. She's found a new home in Canoga Park in the Valley, a three-bedroom apartment where she and Bernard, Jasmine and I, and Monte's son Chase all live together. But caring for Monte is a Herculean task. He hates his meds and does everything he can to avoid taking them. In truth, they are overmedicating him but none of us know to question this back then, none of us understands this, not even Monte. It will be years and multiple hospital visits later before he will tell me that the medication steals him from himself. All it does is make him sleep and be dull. He cannot think on it or create or, in any real way, be in the world.

But it is this Patrisse who greets my father when he gets out from that long stretch locked up. I am still young, but I am a woman now with an analysis and profound real-world responsibilities. I am determined to make up for all the time we lost, as though that were really possible. We go back to seeing each other each weekend, sometimes more. We grow closer than ever and it's not only how Gabriel shows up at events, at meetings and art showcases.

It's also that we are back with the family, my aunties and uncles and cousins and Grandma Vina. I see so much of myself in this side of my family. And it's not just that we look the same. It's that we have the same loud laugh. We dance. I am elated to be back in their bosom. And I bring my friends along—Mark Anthony and Carla and so many others. They're all there in the park with my family, watching the baseball games and eating barbeque and making noise and demonstrating proudly just what love and community look like in action.

And the quality of the conversations with my father goes deeper than it has before. Although I had been to 12-step meetings with him, now that he's older, he talks about what living the life felt like. He says his real addiction is to the fast-paced energy of it all. How else was a man like him ever going to have some money in his pocket, decent clothes, be viewed as someone who mattered? He was invisible before immersing himself in the life, he said. But drugs not only made him feel seen and relevant, the lifestyle itself gave him that sense. My father, a poor Southern boy, was made fun of all his life until he had money in his pocket and a product people wanted.

This is what he is really trying to 12-step around, he says to me one afternoon. An addiction to a lifestyle. He is working hard, once again, to hold himself accountable, which stirs the question in me: Who has ever been accountable to Black people or to my father, a man the world always presented with limited choices? My father attended schools that did little more than train him to serve another man's dreams, ensure another man's wealth, produce another man's vision. The schooling available to my parents' generation did not encourage creativity, the fostering of dreams, the watering of the seeds of hope. Only service.

For my father that service showed up as enlisting in the military. As a young man he would do his time in the army. He tells me he once dreamed of going to college, but that option wasn't real the older he grew. The army was a sure bet, he tells me, providing income for his family. I wanted to relieve the burden Grandma Vina felt, he says one afternoon when we are sitting outside having a brown-bag lunch together. With all the children, it was hard, he says. But it was also hard, he confesses, to leave his siblings behind.

I felt like they were mine, the ones who came after me. The army seemed the best bet, so off I went, my father says, and I think I hear his voice crack. He shrugs for sure. What choice did he have?

What Gabriel does not say but what I am keenly aware of is that when he returned from his tours in Panama and Korea, he returned to a city under siege, economic and otherwise. The GI Bill was notoriously unhelpful to Black veterans, indeed having been forged in such a way as to uphold Jim Crow. And while some gains were made in a post–legal segregation society, it was never a tool men like my father could usefully wield. Anyway, school, which is what it would have covered, was not on his radar. He went, like so many others, just looking for work.

But of course Black Los Angeles in 1984, the year of his discharge, is experiencing rates of unemployment that rival those for Black people in apartheid South Africa. When the economy begins to bounce back, African Americans are extraneous material, discarded, unconsidered in the emerging tech revolution. When Silicon Valley first emerges, it might as well be a Nordic country for all its homogeneity. Even today, its diversity has not yet found a way to reach into the communities of those who were legally and willfully excluded from the paid labor market.

But what is at the ready for us, and on every corner, is access to underground drug markets and all the violence that comes when brothers on the street, or presidents of nations, are defending their territory. My father, Gabriel Brignac, had no territory to defend, only trauma and depression to manage, along with a habit I will believe until the day I die he picked up as a serviceman. Surges in Americans' preferred drugs of choice seem to always align with what is available in the region our nation is invading.

But my father, with no defenders or language that could

dissect the harm done to him, is out there in the mix, a sus-
tenance drug seller and a regular drug user. He is left to
fend for himself. I try continually to talk to my father about
structural realities, policies and decisions as being even
more decisive in the outcomes of his life than any choice he
personally made. I talk about the politics of personal responsibility, how it's mostly a lie meant to keep us from chal-
lenging real-world legislative decisions that chart people's
paths, that undo people's lives.

It was easy to understand that when race was a blatant
factor, a friend says to me in a political discussion one afternoon. Jim Crow left no questions or confusion. But now that
race isn't written into the law, she says, look for the codes.
Look for the coded language everywhere, she says. They re-
wrote the laws, but they didn't rewrite white supremacy.
They kept that shit intact, she says.

I don't know if I ever convince my father of this line of
thinking. A decade of 12-stepping has ensured that he only
really knows how to hold himself accountable. Even with
all my speeches and his engagement with me at the Strategy
Center, I sense when we talk that everyone and everything
else kind of gets a pass.

For this reason we spend most of our time focusing on
the here and the now. My father wants to re-center himself
with me, in his life, in the world at large. He gets a job driving a cement truck and comes to meet me each day for our
brown-bag lunch. And, often with my friends in tow, we
go back to our every weekend spent together. Yes it is the

barbeque and baseball, but it's also Grandma and gumbo, football and family.

We are stitched back together, our Brignac clan and company, a patchwork community brimming with possibility in a small LA apartment ruled by a tiny Creole woman with a fourth-grade education who survived Jim Crow hatred and vicious rapes and unconscionable poverty and brutal domestic violence so she could sit on the other side of it all and still know more than most who have had so much more than she ever did, that at the end of the day, from love we come. To love we must return.

Sometimes I still go to 12-step meetings with Gabriel. Older now, I know I am not only beginning to understand the complexity of human beings and society, but I am sure that the binary that makes a person either good or bad is a dangerously false one for the widest majority of people. I am beginning to see how more than a single truth can live at the same time and in the same person. I can see how my father could have loved my mother but have been in such pain, such self-doubt, that he would not show up that day when she wanted to tell him she was pregnant with me. We talk about compassion, forgiveness, about wanting to heal.

And we talk about me, the breadth of my life, what I dream about and care about—building a new world. I talk about my developing spirituality, my journey to understand God. I never come out and say to my father that I am Queer but neither do I feel as though I have to hide it or myself. We just don't discuss romance much because, well, it's weird. He's my dad regardless. But my friends and my lifestyle make my Queerness pretty obvious and he couldn't care less. He just wants to roll with me. And this, I realize, is what his family cherishes in him. This total absence of judgment. He's easygoing as hell, the original live-and-let-live man. His warmth runs over you like the waters in the hot springs of Central California, enveloping and clean and what you want more and more and more of. In a world that has deliberately made Black humanity invisible, I feel seen in a way that is almost shocking. Is it safe to be all out there like this? And before that thought can settle in my bones, I realize what my father gives me, how he sees me, is necessary as air.

For three years this is who we are. This is our life.

And then Gabriel disappears. Again.

He stops answering my phone calls and he does not call me.

But this time I am not a child. This time I am an adult. I am an organizer. I have survived his incarceration and I have survived Monte's. I have survived homelessness and homophobia. I have chosen dignity and power. I have chosen not to break. I go in search of my dad.

I start hanging around the boarding house he lives in. I call him repeatedly. I call his friends. Fifteen calls, 20 calls, 30 calls, 35 and finally, finally, my father answers the phone. His voice sounds funny but I push and I push: Dad, where are you? I've started calling him Dad.

My father pauses and breathes deep and then he tells me I can find him in the rundown hotel around the corner from

where he lives. I rush over there, annoyed the place hadn't
already occurred to me.

Dad, what the hell? I demand to know when he opens
the door to his room.

But he can barely answer me. All of him is sagging. From
his bones on the inside to his skin on the outside, he's a man
gone limp. I don't know whether to be angry or to be
brokenhearted.

I'm sorry, my father says quietly, his voice threadbare
as tears begin to roll down my cheeks.

I love this man so much. I do not want to lose him. This
is all I can think about it. Stay with me, Dad. Don't leave
me. Don't leave me please.

As always, he is gentle with me. But there is also a stillness to him that comes as a surprise. I don't want to call it
peace. It is not peace. But there is a stillness and also a deep
well of sadness. In that room my father, like me, begins
to cry.

He tells me is embarrassed, ashamed.

He tells me he caught another case and is awaiting trial.
That's why I hadn't been able to reach him. He was in jail
and for the moment, he's out on bail.

They want to give me seven years, he says ever so slowly,
and those words hang there, a blade on a guillotine ready
to sever us from ourselves.

There is nothing about you I am not willing to know, I
say to my father. My father who taught me to live beyond
judgment.

He tells me how much he hated driving that damn cement truck.

He tells me how much he hates himself.

He tells me what it was to come to LA from Louisiana when he was nine years old, a boy with the thick pull of Cajun Country in his voice and manner, marking him as *other* among children seeking tribe. He tells me about being bullied, about how he felt ugly for the whole of his life. He tells me how he cannot remember ever feeling good about himself. He says he never did find a way to learn how to love himself.

We sit with that for a time. What it means to not have the ability to love yourself. How do you honor something you do not love?

That night we speak of prisons and the drug war and how it feels to not seem to matter as a person in the world. He has never been worth saving, never worth treatment.

No intervention beyond prison for this Black man from Louisiana.

We talk about how Black people's relationships are too often defined by harm. We wonder what it means to have so much of our own relationships formed by absence. What goes unsaid, what goes unknown, even as we try to be entirely open before each other? We acknowledge that he has spent more time behind bars and away from me than he has spent time with me.

In this small tattered place, my precious father is high as fuck and drunk.

I have never seen him high before but I refuse to turn away. If he matters to me at all then he has to matter to me at every moment. He has to matter to me at this moment. Seeing him like this feels like my soul is being pulled over shards of glass but I do not turn away. His life is not expendable. Our love is not disposable. I will not be to him what the world has been to him. I will not throw him away. I will not say he has nothing to offer.

I tell him that relapse is a part of recovery.

I ask, What if we wrote off every person who fell off a diet? We laugh at that, but just briefly.

My father's addiction and the stigma that attaches to it have made him so deeply lonely, forced him into a world that cannot ever be fully shared by anyone who loves him. I love him. I tell him I want to share his whole life with him. He sighs and expels air. He deflates. I move closer to him. He lets me. I tell him I won't leave him and I don't. We talk or we don't, for the rest of the night. We hold each other on and off. We cry.

Two months later my father is sentenced to three years in prison. He is able to avoid the seven-year bid because he volunteers to go to the prison fire camp, a program where convicts are made to serve as frontline first responders when the California wildfires break out. They are the ones who go in before trained firefighters do.

My father risks death for a faster shot at freedom.

It is 2009 and I am 26 years old when Gabriel comes home from prison.

He will never go back again.

We—me, Mark Anthony and Carla—pool our little bit of money and fly him home from Northern California, where he had been held in the fire prison camp. Mark Anthony and I have become a couple in the intervening years and Carla and I, we are best friends still. We meet him at the airport. It is the first time I am seeing my father since he was taken away and in this time I have grown this small family around me, around us.

As they did with Monte, almost a decade before and in all the years since my brother came home, my friends have invested themselves in my father's and my life, and their love has helped stop the bleeding when our spirits were caught in all that concertina wire, the wounds that went past the sinew and bone, laid claim to the marrow. My community of friends, this chosen family of mine, loves in a way that sets an example for love. Their love as a triumph, as a breathing and alive testimony to what we mean when we say another world is possible.

My father emerges from the gate area and I squeal like I am a child of five and run to him. The joy I feel in my body is so alive and pulsing. I swear it is something everyone can see. And I cannot stop holding my father and he cannot stop holding me and this is how we are and this is how we stay in the middle of LAX until finally my dad says softly, Anyone hungry? I'm starving. And we pile into Carla's car.

For a week my father lives with me, sleeping on my couch, but he wants his independence, he wants to not be a burden. He moves into a shelter, which allows him to feel more independent. He begins 12-stepping again and applies for Section 8 so he can get permanent, secure housing. Years after I first suggested it, my father finally determines to get his CASAC—Credentialed Alcohol and Substance Abuse Counselor—certificate. He wants to spend the rest of his life helping people heal.

He enrolls in the program at Pierce College in LA while I enroll at UCLA. I am the first person on my mother's side of the family to attend college. We are a father and daughter determined to write our own history and it's March now and all we can see is the sun rising higher and brighter. We live in gratitude and hope and then June arrives and word comes that his father has died.

Dad gets permission from his parole officer to travel, and we take a trip to our ancestral home in Eunice, Louisiana, a city of fewer than 11,000, known for Cajun music. The last time I was there, the only time I was there, was four years before in the wake of Katrina. After delivering food and supplies along the devastated Gulf Coast, I went to meet my grandfather, who welcomed me into his home, made me a meal, told me I look like the Brignacs going back gen-erations. Me with my wide mouth and big forehead. They come from a place. I come from a place.

This trip to Eunice with my father is more healing than sad, despite the occasion. And for the first time in my life I see my father at complete ease. I have never seen this side of him before. There's something in his walk, in his smile. Nothing is heavy. Nothing is forced. We walk all through the town that he lived in until he was nine. I see places where he played as a boy. We sit with family on porches. We watch sunsets. We talk shit, we play the dozens. We eat and we eat. We tell family stories and stand up while we do it. We clap. We are loud. We love each other openly and hard.

The funeral for my grandfather is held in the single church in the neighborhood, a Baptist one, and in that house of worship we mourn but we know we will survive because Eunice teaches us this, that all our bones matter, that all the broken pieces of us somehow make a whole.

Dad, I think you should move here, I say. You seem so happy in this place, so at peace, I say.

Too slow for me here, he argues back and praises LA, the city for him that made freedom an ever-moving target.

After a week we say goodbye to Eunice, to my Grandfather Carl, to porches and slow walks and ongoing spaces of Black people who just love you and openly. Together, we head back to LA, and I spend much of the summer watching my father play baseball with his brothers, the game he loves, surrounded by the people he loves.

By now I am fully in love with Mark Anthony, who is patient and kind and deeply consistent. He is not insecure about my previous relationships, in particular ones I've had with women. He does not judge my sexuality. He loves me as is, which is a gift I wish for all of us to receive, the gift of being loved simply because of who you are, not in spite of it, not with condition, not loved in parts.

Mark Anthony is a man who has literally dedicated himself to healing; while I am in religious studies at UCLA, he is doing his master's in Chinese medicine. A friend's mother has a tiny cottage in Topanga Canyon that's surrounded by trees. We decide to move in together. The area is more breathtakingly beautiful than any I've ever lived in up to that point and I accept, finally, that this is my life, this is my blessed life as the winter holidays roll in. I tell my father we will celebrate them fully. All those moments we missed together, we will make up for them this year. On Thanksgiving my Grandma Vina will make gumbo with such love that I am filled until Christmas.

On December 25, 2009, my Grandma's house is in full party mode. This is my father's first Christmas back home in half a decade. All the family shows up and before the night comes to a close, between all of us who are gathered, I am certain we say I love you one thousand times. We kiss each other until we spill over in giggles and laugh until we ache. We leave my Grandma's home having wrapped ourselves in ourselves and snuggled down in it. We thank all the universe for the grace shown our family. We say Good Night to one another and we say it very deliberately because on this Christmas in 2009, we give those words such deliberate meaning.

On December 26, I don't speak to my father, which is why I call him early on December 27. I don't reach him but I leave a message, and he calls me back, a call that I miss. He leaves me a voicemail in which he says he doesn't feel well, a message I do not get immediately. I am at my mother's house, visiting. She's had a fight with my sister Jasmine and Mark Anthony and I have come to help patch things up.

We talk, we help settle things and after not so long, we head back up to the Canyon, driving that long stretch of road in which cell service drops out. When we pull up to our small home I hear our landline ringing and now voicemail alerts are coming through on my cell.

I answer the landline.

Are you sitting down? It's my mother and her voice is in a panic.

I tell her I'm not and I ask her what's wrong, but she cannot stop asking me if I am sitting down. She asks me four times, five times and now I've spun into a panic. My mind goes immediately for some reason to my nephew Chase, Monte's now near-teenaged son.

Where's Chase? What's wrong? What is going on? I yell. Mom! What is it?!

Which is when she says it.

They think your father is dead, she says. That's what they're saying.

When you are told that your father is dead you really can't believe it's true, you can't just accept it and I didn't. What proof was there? My mother has heard the news from a cousin who heard it from another man who lived in the shelter that my father lived in. But no one in my family has heard from the shelter itself. I take this as a hopeful sign. I am questioning my mother as I am corralling Mark Anthony to head back down the mountain, out to find my father. I have always been able to find my father. We get into the car and Mark Anthony will recall for me later that I went into shock. I am unable to speak.

He will tell me later of guiding me to the car and into

the passenger's seat so we could begin the 30-minute ride back down the Canyon. I remember clutching my phone. I don't remember why. We cannot get service for the entirety of the ride. When we finally do, I call my father's cell. I call it and call it, trying to will him to answer. Mark Anthony tells me later I was still doing this as we pulled up to the shelter, even as the street was filled with police cars and a van from the coroner's office.

I get out of the car and approach the first officer I see. I'm Gabriel Brignac's daughter. I say this matter-of-factly and equally as matter-of-factly, the officer says to me, Your father is dead. I'm sorry.

The officer tells me I cannot go upstairs to see my father's body until the medical examiner has determined whether or not there was foul play.

I sit outside the shelter unable to move, and then one by one my friends who Mark Anthony has called begin to arrive and surround me. The medical examiner emerges, declares my father's death was not foul play. I am allowed upstairs, this final moment with the man who helped give me life.

My father is on a stretcher in front of the room he shared with three other men.

He is wearing white boxers and a white t-shirt.

He still has on his glasses and his watch.

I remove them. I keep them.

I go into his room and look around this tiny space that once was and now no longer is his, this place where he was reinventing himself. I begin packing up the few material items that proved he was here. My father was here. He existed. Gabriel Brignac. This single lockbox of important papers. These few pairs of shoes and items of clothing. They are not the sum of a man. But they are part of him. I pack them up.

This is the business of death.

I lean over my father's body.

I kiss him one final time.

I tell him I love him.

There is nothing more I can do here. I turn away slowly and just as slowly, I leave.

I want my father to have the dignity in death he was never afforded in life.

I search for a funeral home and a florist. I call everyone in his address book and tell them we are planning the service. The work helps blunt the pain for a time. I select a casket because it is powder blue and my father loved blue. My grandmother selects a suit for him to wear in death that is nicer than any item of clothing my father owned in life.

At the turn of a new year, on January 3, 2010, 300 of us gather to honor the life of Gabriel Brignac. My friend sings *Amazing Grace*.

TWAS GRACE THAT TAUGHT MY HEART TO FEAR

AND GRACE MY FEARS RELIEVED

HOW PRECIOUS DID THAT GRACE APPEAR

THE HOUR I FIRST BELIEVED.

I believed in my father.

I believed in Gabriel Brignac.

I believed in us.

I still believe in us.

My father's sponsor rises and assumes the position before the microphone and begins to speak. He tells the room about a man desperate to be a better version of himself. He tells the room of a man who was gentle. He tells the room of a man who worked as hard as any man he knew. He tells the room that my father was just coming up on Steps 8 and 9 in the program. He was making a list of the people he had harmed and then finding ways to make amends to each one.

In that room, on that day, we give my father the Steps 8 and 9.

We choose forgiveness and love as a collective act.

When it is my turn to stand and face this group of people I have gathered, the first time I have ever called community together to acknowledge a life, I am overwhelmed by the responsibility to offer a eulogy that is as authentic as Gabriel Brignac was. I stand and speak of a man who was more brilliant than he knew or was ever given credit for. I tell them about a man who was a full burst of love. I speak about a man who was flawed and flawless, as each one of us is. I speak about a man I am proud to call my father.

A week after the service we drive out to the cemetery in Riverside, California. We are going to bury my father with complete military honors. There are six of us gathered at this final resting place, including my grandmother and my

Aunt Jackie, who works at the Pentagon. Aunt Jackie is dressed in full uniform and represents her brother with a deep swell of pride. And her brother—a forgotten veteran of wars he never knew had been declared on his one thin brown body that in the end would succumb to a heart that was broken. My father, at 50 years old, officially died of a heart attack.

We sit before his casket as "Taps" begins to play and a soldier presents me with the folded American flag that had covered his coffin. I take it and I hold it, this flag for a nation in which my father, my Black father, my good and imperfect and loving Black father, could not be possible.

My father who got cages instead of compassion.

My father whose whole story no one of us will ever know.

What did it do to him, all those years locked away, all that time in chains, all those days upon days without human touch except touch meant to harm—*hands behind your back, Nigger. Get on the fucking wall, Nigger! Lift your sac, Nigger. Don't look at me like that or I will fucking kill your Black ass.*

It would be easy to speculate about the impact of years of cocaine use on my father's heart, but I suspect that it will tell us less than if we could measure the cumulative effects of hatred, racism and indignity. What is the impact of years of strip searches, of being bent over, the years before that when you were a child and knew that no dream you had for yourself was taken seriously by anyone, that you were not someone who would be fully invested in by a nation that treated you as expendable?

What is the impact of not being valued?

How do you measure the loss of what a human being does not receive?

My father was part of a generation of Black men who spent a lifetime watching hope and dreams shoved just out of their reach until it seemed normal, the way it just was. I lost my father at a time when 2.2 million people had gone missing on our watch, buried in prisons that were buried in small towns, but somehow and unbelievably this man kept coming back.

He kept coming back.

He kept coming back.

And he kept trying. My father kept fucking trying. This man. My father. Gabriel Brignac who loved me deeply and fiercely. Who spent every moment with me telling me how my Black life mattered. This was my father, the bones and the blood and the soul of him. This was Gabriel Brignac and I hold that flag that had covered his casket, this man who died of a broken heart in this nation of broken promises, and I think that if my father could not be possible in this America, then how is it that such a thing as America can ever be possible?

PART TWO

BLACK LIVES MATTER

8

ZERO DARK THIRTY

THE REMIX

*Come celebrate with me that every day something has tried
to kill me and has failed.*

LUCILLE CLIFTON

My phone jolts me out of a deeply needed sleep just
past midnight. It is my mother's voice I hear on the other
end of the line: Trisse, it's your brother, she says. It's Monte.
He's been arrested.

I sit up immediately and try to shake the sleep from my
body, my brain. My exhaustion is encompassing and thick. It
is 2006 and I am in college full time now, studying philoso-
phy with a concentration in the Abrahamic traditions. But
I am also working full time with Mark Anthony and our
friend Jason, executing a special program at my old high
school, Cleveland, on trauma and resilience. It takes me a
minute. Only just a month before they had taken my father,

Gabriel, to the fire camp prison. How do I make sense of what my mother is saying? How do I make sense of a world that seems hell-bent on subverting it?

Monte had come home from his first prison bid in 2003, and as we learned quickly, frighteningly, there was no infrastructure that existed to help secure either his re-entry or his mental health. Whatever was going to happen would happen because of us, the family, and our capacity to manage severe mental illness. We learned quickly that intervention was either us alone and without medical professional support, or it was the police. The brutal memory of Monte's first break, during which we learned that there were no social services or safety nets for my brother, hung over all of our heads like a sword. We lived alongside the steady buzz of anxiety. I turned ever more toward spirit, toward that which I could not see but could feel at all times, in order to manage my emotions. This is to say I prayed often and surrounded myself ever more closely with the family I'd created. Mark Anthony and Tanya, a close friend from high school. Jason from work. New friends from the Strategy Center. They sustained me.

When Monte came home, after we were able to get him stable after weeks in the hospital, he wanted nothing more than to be a self-sufficient man in the world. But the cycling in and out of juvie during his childhood—for drinking or tagging or just standing on the street with his boys—and then of course the time in prison, meant he had never had a single job in his life, save for any forced labor when he was locked up.

We helped him to get a low-wage, low-level job at a local Rite Aid—Carla and I had both done our time at Rite
Aids in LA—and I still remember his excitement at the end
of the first day: Trisse, I got this! He was so deeply proud.
But a week into his very first paid position, he was promptly
fired. His background check had come back: No ex-felons,
dude, get the hell out.

We tried pulling him closer to us, and my mother
begged him to live with her, risking her Section 8 status. If
you have government housing benefits you cannot have anyone living with you if they've been convicted of a crime.
Even if they are a juvenile. And even if they are incapable
of caring for themselves because of an illness. And even if
they cannot get a job because even the most low-level jobs
won't hire someone with a conviction. In California there
are more than 4,800 barriers to re-entry, from jobs, housing and food bans, to school financial aid bans and the list
goes on. You can have a two-year sentence but it doesn't
mean you're not doing life.

In any case, Monte didn't want to put my mother at risk
and decided instead, and against our wishes, to move back
in with Cynthia, the mother of his son Chase. But Cynthia
had her own set of challenges in managing life since she had
been shot all those years ago and left paralyzed. Some were
physical and some were emotional and all were present. My
mother, in fact, stepped in to be Chase's caretaker because
of his mother's overwhelm and my brother's own struggles.
But disabled and poor and never having had treatment for
the PTSD borne of having her life nearly taken at only

18 years old, Cynthia was in no position to manage Monte and ensure he took his medication or get him to County USC hospital to see a doctor who could check to see that his levels were maintained.

And like many people who struggle with schizoaffective disorder—a diagnosis that includes bipolar disorder—Monte eventually began to feel he was fine, he was better, in fact, without the medications. We didn't know this at first but when we began to see signs of erratic behavior—his mood was exaggerated, too excited, he was speaking too fast—my mother, Paul and I pushed him to come with us to a doctor.

Monte, you need medical support, I tried to convince my brother. All of us do. But my brother's primary engagement with doctors had been in prison, a sure way to destabilize if not completely destroy their relationship to healing. Even later, after he was home and we got him into County USC, medical staff treated him, a poor Black man from a poor Black family, a man with a conviction, not as a person whose critical condition could put him at the top of their list. They were perfunctory, in part because of their overwhelm, I'm sure. They did not remember his name or ours. There was no time for bedside pleasantries and reassurances. Get him in, get him stabilized and get him the fuck out. Somebody else needs this bed. For my brother, hospitals signaled harm if not outright hatred: Monte knew they didn't care for him and were not even particularly invested in seeing him well, only contained, controlled.

But in these predawn hours in the spring of 2006, my

mother tells me she doesn't know the details, that she got a call from Monte but he was neither clear nor calm. We cannot do anything to help Monte until later in the morning. I tell my mother that we'll head to Twin Towers, the LA County Jail that I assume is holding my brother, first thing in the morning.

Monte is not in Twin Towers, my mother informs me.

Whatever happened, she says, Monte's in the hospital. We have to go see him there.

There's a fear that grips you, a vise, a garrote, when you are entering a place that is unknown, unknowable. And yes, in these times there can be bursts of relief: perhaps the ending will be one that is an alternative to the terrible ones you cannot help but imagine. But I know no such feeling now, in our own zero dark thirty, in our family's own treacherous theater of war, which in this moment has anchored itself against my brother, a man trying to live in a world that refuses a relationship with him that is not rooted in pain.

When Paul, my mother and I head to the hospital, our sister, Jasmine, does not join us. Seeing Monte in the condition we fear he will be in is too much for her to bear. I approach the hospital in the full expanse of prayer, a calling to every God and Goddess I have ever heard of or known.

Ogún oko dara obaniché aguanile ichegún iré.
(Warrior for justice, protect my brother.)

In Monte's County USC hospital room, which is located in the prison wing, he is being guarded by two members of the Los Angeles Police Department. Before we enter the room they nonchalantly tell me pieces of my brother's story:

We thought he was on PCP or something, one says.

He's mentally ill, I respond, and wonder why cops never seem to think that Black people can have mental illness.

He's huge! one exclaims. Massive! They had to use rubber bullets on him, one says, casually, like he's not talking about my family, a man I share DNA with. Like it's a motherfucking video game to them.

We had to tase him too, the other cop offers, like tasing doesn't kill people, like it couldn't have killed my brother.

I will learn later that my brother had been driving and had gotten into a fender bender with another driver, a white woman, who promptly called the police. My brother was in an episode and although he never touched the woman or did anything more than yell, although his mental illness was as clear as the fact that he was Black, he was shot with rubber bullets and tased.

And then he was charged with terrorism.

Literally.

If someone alleges that you have said something threatening to them and causing them to fear for their life, you can be charged, as my brother, who was in a full manic episode, was charged, with terrorism.

When we at last talk to Monte, his words are unclear and slurry. We cannot understand him and then eventually he begins crying uncontrollably. This is the other side of a manic episode, this brutal drop down the darkest hole, something deeper than sadness, an aching and hopelessness that finds home at a cellular level. We cannot make out almost anything he is saying except this one simple plea: Can I have medication please? I don't feel well, please?

The horror of this disease is that at one stage your brain will trick you into believing that you are well, more than well—that you are better than anyone ever has been. In this phase you believe that you don't need your medication. And then without warning and often without a perceptible trigger, you're in your own personal hell that no one can snatch you out of.

Two days later Monte is transferred to Twin Towers as a high-power alert prisoner, which means he is classified as a threat to officers. To hear this is complete cognitive fucking dissonance: my brother has never hurt another living being, let alone a cop. But he has been stripped, beaten and starved, kicked and humiliated by cops. So they get to call him the threat. They get to call him the harm. They get to charge him with terrorism.

Incarcerated as a high-power alert prisoner, Monte is kept in his cell 23 hours a day in solitary confinement, a condition that has long been proven to instigate mental illness in those who previously had been mentally stable. In my brother's case, he deteriorates quickly, predictably, horribly and without a single doctor on that staff to assert the Oath: first do no harm. When I go to Twin Towers for the first time to visit my brother, he makes the plea again.

I don't feel well, Trisse. Can I please have my meds?

They giving me Advil but I need my meds. Please Trisse.
Please.

His voice, the look in eyes, breaks my heart. I wonder
if heart meds are withheld from people, cancer meds, an
asthma pump? We know Hep C treatments are. And nal-
oxone, which can reverse an OD, has been. We certainly
know meds that would slow the onset of AIDS have been
kept out of reach of certain groups of people. What kind of
society uses medicine as a weapon, keeps it from people
needing to heal, all the while continuing to develop the
drugs America's prisons use to execute people?

Even still I cannot figure out why it works in the jailers'
interest to withhold treatment for my brother. They're the
ones who diagnosed him in the first place! They have all of
his records! I tell him I will get him whatever he needs, and
I talk to the sheriff, who for some moment I assume will be
reasonable. I mean, isn't a properly medicated Monte better for everyone? The sheriff blows me off after I argue and
argue. Can't authorize nothing without the doctor and the
doc didn't give the word, he repeats. And then I get it. The
cheaper alternative to medicating Monte is strapping him
down in five-point restraints in a room by himself. Reduces
the cost of not only the medication itself, but guards and
likely food.

The second time I go to see Monte I am turned away.
He's not fit to be seen, an officer tells me. I go back and go
back each of his scheduled visitation days and each time
I am turned away, as is our mother. We will not have an op-

portunity to lay eyes on Monte again until his court date arrives, some 21 days after his arrest. We turn out in full force, not just Mom and me and the family, but Mark Anthony; my colleague from Cleveland, Jason; and other friends of ours in a show of support.

At the court I approach the bailiff to ensure Monte's on the docket.

Monte Cullors? she asks.

Yes, I say.

She looks over some materials and disappears for a moment and then returns and looks me in my face.

I want to warn you: your brother is in really bad condition. It's very alarming.

Her affect is flat. I don't know what to think.

What do you mean, I ask?

He's on a gurney, she says. She pauses.

He is strapped down, she continues. Restrained, she says.

And also, she continues, using the same flat tone, his face is covered with a spit net, she concludes.

This woman, who perhaps has a brother or perhaps has a son or perhaps has loved somebody's brother or son, is almost as nonchalant as the officer who told me my brother had been shot with rubber bullets and tased.

My mouth is agape. I'm in shock. I'm trying to process what I cannot imagine. They are going to have my brother hemmed up like he's Hannibal fucking Lecter? How is it possible that the only response we have for poor people who are mentally ill is criminalization? How does this align with the notion of a democratic or free society—to not take care of *the least of these?* More mentally ill people in our nation's prisons than in all of our psychiatric hospitals—combined?! Human beings charged with all manner of terrible-sounding crimes—terrorism!—like my brother has been. What kind of society do we live in?

And, like my brother, many have never harmed another being.

And even those who have harmed others—what if there had been appropriate interventions, medical interventions, compassionate interventions, early on? What if we, if all of us, had access to health care that centered the patient, not the money? Systems like this actually exist on this planet, in this time. Why is America so tethered to punishment and judgment, to one life mattering and another not? I am thinking of all the people, like my brother, like my father—who have been the targets of harm, not the harm itself. And yet they are the ones whom society views as disposable. Our nation, one big damn *Survivor* reality nightmare. I am filled with a sense of rage and a call to action at the idea that my brother, my Monte, is considered someone disposable to these people. But to me and my mother and to my sister and my brother, to Chase and to Cynthia, Monte was never disposable. Not him nor the measure of his great heart or beautiful broken brain, which perhaps wrestles so mightily because my God, how the fuck does any of this make sense?

Why is he here? I demand to know. Why isn't he getting treatment? Jesus, what is wrong with you people?

The bailiff doesn't answer me and I return to my seat in this court where you cannot speak or use a cell phone or do anything but pray and pray.

Obatalá obá layé ela iwo alara, Ache.

There is suddenly a disturbance, and I look up, we all do, which is when we see what has been done to my brother. Monte is in a full psychotic break. He is yelling and talking to himself. Monte's presence in the courtroom is roughly the equivalent of dragging someone before a judge who has just been shot in the face and expecting that that person will somehow be able to be an active participant in the proceedings. It's a stunning betrayal of human dignity, of the words And Justice for All.

Again.

We should be used to this, I should be used to this. But I can never get used to this. I refuse to.

My mother begins to cry and Jason holds her close as Mark Anthony takes my hand in his own and squeezes it. To one side of me and just in front, three white men who are also in the court, I suppose for their family member or friend, begin to laugh. No one silences them. They look at my brother as though he is the freak show. They look at him as though he is not a human being.

I am gripped with an encompassing sense of shame and humiliation. I don't want to feel this way but here is all of our family's pain on full blast before people who hate us. I try to stay centered, to say with my eyes, which are laser-focused on Monte, what the court will not allow me to say with my mouth. I love you Monte. I am coming for you. I won't let them take you, baby. Just stay with me, Monte. Stay with me.

I have to fight back the urge to run to my brother. It's a particular kind of evil, a specific sort of sadism, when someone forces you to be still and silent while a person you love is hurting just beyond your reach and in ways that can never fully be measured. I am desperate to go to him, to hold my brother, this brother who held me as a child, this brother who rescued and fed small animals, this brother I so love.

And then the judge walks in. She assesses the situation: a man in a face mask and five-point restraints tethered to a gurney who is yelling gibberish and fighting to get free. Perplexed, she speaks to the bailiff who is acting as though there is something normal, something fine about the situation.

The judge then asks publicly, Why is this man in the courtroom? No one has an answer. Not the bailiff, not the DA, not Monte's public defender, who hasn't said word one in my brother's defense. He almost looks distracted, the way he keeps glancing at his watch and the papers before him.

In a voice all of us can hear, the judge admonishes the cops who brought Monte in, the DA and the public defender. And then she postpones my brother's date. The cops almost shrug and move to roll Monte and his gurney back out of the courtroom. And as they do, Monte yells one last thing, dragging a simple, one-syllable word out for what felt like a full minute. For what felt like a final, desperate prayer: *MOM!!!!!!!!!!!!!!!!!!!!!*

We leave the courtroom, silent in our procession. We are in shock. We are aliens traversing a strange and hostile planet. We are survivors crawling from the wreckage of a crash scene and we are bruised, broken in parts, bleeding. But we are still breathing. I am still breathing and after a short time, the stunned sensation that took hold of my body, my soul, begins to erode, transform. I am angry, so angry, and I find I have to summon all the strength within me to try not to explode. I turn to Monte's ineffective public defender.

How dare you allow that to happen? How could you not even try to stop them from putting Monte and our family through that?

He shrugs. If he said anything, I can no longer remember. Who is this guy and why does he present himself as part of Monte's team? He has nothing to offer in this moment, no word let alone a plan. In another space and time I might have some sympathy for his overwhelm. He's clearly in a place he's never been. But so are we. I turn away from him and toward my mother, my mother who has spent a lifetime sharpening her reserve into a weapon against the attacks of the world. That weapon has come apart in this courthouse and now she is crying without restraint. She is sobbing. She chokes out these words: I feel so guilty.

I'm confused. Why would my mother, our mother, feel

guilty? What did she ever do except love us and work for us, two, three jobs at a time, and worship and follow rules, while her own family turned its back on her? And then slowly I begin to consider: Is this what it is to be a mother who has to carry the weight of having to protect her children in a world that is conspiring to kill them? Are you forced to exist within a terrible trinary of emotion: rage, grief or guilt? What of the joy and the peace that loving a child brings? What of pride and of hope? Could it really be true that my mother has been given no door number four or five or six or even seven to walk through in order to know the wholeness of motherhood? Is she one in a long line of Black mothers limited to survival mode or grief?

Has my mother ever been allowed to lose herself in the laughter of her children, the silly baby games, the simple adolescent struggles—do your homework, do your chores? I do not remember ever going to a movie with my mother, window shopping. I do not remember us together as relaxed, as humans *being*. We have always had to be humans *doing*.

Is this my mother who is gripped, albeit wrongly, with guilt? Is she in this moment wondering what she did or did not do to ensure her baby, her Monte, be kept safe from the nightmare he's been cast into? Is my mother the fallout, the collateral damage in the battle to elevate personal responsibility over everything, over all those decisions that were made about state budget priorities, about wages, about the presence of police, and even about damn grocery stores and access to quality food?

Here, in this hour and in this place, in this system of law

that is supposed to be adversarial but is instead where the players all side up against her son, my mother accesses the only feeling she'd ever been allowed to access freely. Guilt.

Guilt for having a baby young.

Guilt for not blindly following patriarchal religious protocols.

Guilt for being poor.

Guilt for not keeping mental illness out of her son's brain.

Guilt that she could not stop a group of people from divorcing themselves from a useful definition of humanity.

Guilt that she could not keep these moral monsters from harming her baby.

I put my arms around my precious mother.

It's not your fault, Mom, I say. None of this is. Not his illness and not what it looks like when it goes untreated. It's not your fault, it's not your fault, I keep saying, I keep affirming this with her. But I don't know whether or not she actually believes me. I didn't know then and I don't know now.

Another court date is set and in advance of that, in the courthouse, Mom and I meet with the public defender. We never do get to meet with him in an office, a place we can think and strategize together. We are allowed these few minutes on a bench in a hallway.

Right off the PD tells us that this case represents my brother's third strike and Monte will be sentenced to life in prison. Full stop.

Monte's first arrest for an attempted breaking and en-

tering while he was in the middle of an episode was his first
strike. While he was incarcerated, guards claimed to find a
weapon in his cell. Monte denied it was his and we never
knew about this, but regardless, he was convicted and there-
fore: strike two. This third incident in which the charge is
terrorism, also in the midst of an episode where he yelled
and carried on *but threatened no one and hurt no one,* represents strike three and that's it. He qualifies for a living death
sentence and that's fucking that. The public defender is non-
plussed as he says this, and he is not embarrassed that he
has no plan to fight back. He says this is what Monte wants.
He literally said that.

Go tell my brother we're hiring a lawyer, I order, and
he disappears through a door, back where I suppose the
holding cells are kept, where my brother is being kept. He
comes back quickly. Your brother says don't worry about it.

Now I hiss: Go. Tell. My. Brother. We. *ARE.* Hiring. A.
Lawyer.

Full damn stop.

This time when he disappears and returns, he is compliant. Is that humility I read on his face, I wonder?

Your brother says fine, he informs my family. He says
it's okay to find a lawyer and that he might know someone,
he mutters.

We're done here, I tell my mother. Being an organizer,
volunteering with the Strategy Center, has made me bold.
Fuck this loser. There is another way. Now we have only to
find the money, which is a mountain that shoots up, its apex
beyond where I can see if I use only these two human eyes.

This moment requires a sight born of faith, of walk-on-water faith.

It's the faith that drove us to run without maps or compasses, money or friends, with dogs trained by demons following behind. It's the faith that sent four Black students, on February 1, 1960, Joseph McNeil, Franklin Mc-Cain, David Richmond and Ezell Blair, to sit down at a "whites-only" lunch counter at a Woolworth's in Greensboro, North Carolina, and refuse to move, risking bodily harm and their very lives. It's the faith that allowed Robert Parris Moses to keep pushing for voting rights in the deep South in 1965 despite only being able to register one Black man that first summer in Amite County, Mississippi.

The stories I learned as a small girl who read about civil rights and Black power and Black culture flowed everywhere in me and through me. The lessons I'd learned from the Strategy Center about how to organize in the face of unrelenting odds had taken full root.

The court hearing is perfunctory: a new date is set. We have two weeks to hire and finance a private attorney. Facebook exists only at Harvard at this point. There's MySpace but no architecture for digital crowd-funding campaigns. There's no Twitter. I go to visit Monte, who tells me another prisoner has recommended a really good attorney whose name is Peter Corn. Even still, Monte's not hopeful.

Trisse, he says, I'm going to be here until Armageddon comes, he says.

I tell him he won't be. I tell him we will fix this. And then I go to meet this Peter Corn guy, who immediately makes me feel uncomfortable. But there's not much choice. We need $10,000. I have maybe $150 in my bank account. My mother is still paid poverty wages. And it's going to be up to my mother and I. Alton isn't reliable; he has money, just doesn't dish it out. Paul and Jasmine are feeling overwhelmed by both Monte's illness and the attacks by the court. Who can blame them? What supports are there, what therapy, what road map is offered, when one of your own is being lynched in your presence and you have no army to fight back with, no gun, no Underground Railroad? This is the way it is set up: to intimidate families and shut them down and away from the people they love the most when those very people most need support.

But I refuse to be intimidated.

I have been an organizer since I was 16 years old.

From my teacher and friends at Cleveland I learned that just because I was young, it did not mean I couldn't be a leader. Cleveland taught us, taught me, that leadership was our responsibility.

From the Strategy Center I learned how to map a campaign with young Black and Brown people, and that we could actually win that campaign. Monte's arrest came the year we won a fight against the school district for fining parents $250 each time their child was late to school—even if they were late because the lines to get through the metal detectors were unconscionably long.

Donna taught me to know faith, to understand spirit as a verb.

And from my intentional family—Mark Anthony and Carla, Naomi and Tanya and Jason and Sarah and Katidia and Vitaly and more people than I can name here, I learned that nothing could break a community united, a community guided by love. From them, I learned to reimagine a world. A world where my own family can be safe. A world where Monte can be safe. I learned that I am not alone no matter how lonely I'd felt at times.

No problem, I say to Peter Corn. We'll have your retainer in two weeks. And then I go to work. We go to work.

My friends, my people, my tribe, take to making calls and writing letters, which we email and snail mail out. And then we pray. And then we wait. But not for long. Within ten days checks from across the country begin to pour in and days before I have to pay Peter Corn, we have $6,000 raised.

I ask my mother to go to her father, to her middle-class family. Ask them for the balance, Mom.

They'll say no, she's sure.

Ask anyway, I insist. And she does. And after fits and starts and an interminable two days of silence, my grandparents send over the final $4,000. I go to meet Peter Corn.

At his office that day, his partner is there and he listens in. When he hears my brother's name, he asks if we are related to a man named Rodney Cullors.

Yes, I say. He's our uncle, I say.

Small world, he declares. I prosecuted him once.

There's an awkward pause. I try not to be derailed by the fact that for these folks, this is all a chess game. They can play the pieces on any side of the board. I try to be comforted by the idea that at least they will know how to come at the prosecutors, and they do. Peter says immediately: We gotta strike one of the strikes. Probably won't avoid any prison at all (I seethe) but we can get around life. This whole process unnerves me. Is it ever really about defending people or is it always only about getting the better deal? This is what we're forced into.

Peter Corn is true to his word—and has remained so for Monte over the course of the years we've known him. He gets the second strike struck, the one Monte was given while he was in prison, but Monte has to plead out and agree to serve 85 percent of an eight-year sentence. No one mentions medical treatment or what the proper response to a person who is unwell should be. Somehow we feel something like grateful. Not really grateful. But something like it. I begin visiting my brother every month, a process I continue for the six years he ends up serving at Corcoran State Prison, where they find the right balance of meds to keep Monte mostly together.

Six months before Monte comes home, I tell Mark Anthony, whom I have dated on and off for years, but am now fully committed to, that we cannot allow what happened before. Monte needs a re-entry team, I whisper one night, laying in Mark Anthony's loving arms. The next day we put out a call to people from the Strategy Center, my friends Tanya, Jason and Carla. I reach out to mentors. I try to convince my mother to let me find a home for Monte that will support his transition but she will hear none of it.

My son will live with me, she says, and that's it.

In October of 2011, Alton, Paul and I rise at 4:00 in the morning and load into my dad's monster truck, an F-350, to begin the three-hour drive up 99 North. Monte will not be sent home alone on a bus again, in his underwear. As we pull up into the dawn of the day at the prison, I see workers, as if for the first time. They are gardening, mowing the lawn, doing all sorts of tasks. And they are all in prison jumpsuits. Prisoners are literally an enslaved workforce, not only to external companies like Starbucks and Whole Foods, but to the state of California itself. The prison provides jobs in the town for guards and nurses, a couple of counselors. But not for janitors, cooks, people who make the furniture. These are all parts of America's sprawling slave labor system. Just then, a single white van pulls up and a group of men step out. Monte is among them.

He is wearing the 501 jeans we sent him, black Stacy Adams shoes and a trademark Ese black shirt. Alton begins to weep and Monte says with a laugh, Smile now, cry later old man, and they embrace.

Monte turns to me and exclaims: Trisse! What's up?? He grabs me and Paul into hugs. Standing near Monte is an elder who has no one meeting him and who has nowhere to go. Monte looks at Dad, Hey can he come with us? It's a gentle demand framed as a question. Alton's not thrilled, but this is Monte. We all pile into the van and the elder and Monte stare out of the window. So long since I last saw any of this scenery, Monte says. These colors, he says. The elder doesn't say a word but he doesn't stop staring, either.

Monte shifts and begins playing with the cell phone we've bought him. The world has turned over several times since 2006.

We stop for a bite along the way and are thrilled to watch Monte scarf down chicken, steak, pinto beans and rice. When we get into the Valley, Alton asks the elder, Hey, where should I take you? But the old man has no plan. That much is clear. He is reflective of so many prisoners who are coming home after lengthy sentences. They come home to a world they don't know, to a people who don't know them.

I'm just gonna head down to Hollywood, he says. We take him there and I give him some of the little money I have and get back in the truck, and we head back home to my mother's new Section 8 apartment complete with a small balcony where a barbecue is happening. Chase and Monte reunite awkwardly; Chase won't give his father a full embrace. He's in full-blown adolescence and perhaps that explains part of it, but most of it is about how you can never get back the time.

He's not happy to see me, Monte whispers to me sadly.

Yeah he is, I respond. He just has to get used to things.

We go for a walk that night through the old neighborhood for a little while, we talk or don't, we laugh, we don't cry, we embrace the sense of relative calm. I kiss my mother, my brother at the end of the night.

Call me in the morning, Mom, I say, and she promises she will. Monte walks me to the door. Can you help me find a job, Trisse? I need to work, he says.

He does not yet know that my team and I have already

been planning something for him. There's a small social justice organization I've been working with. They will give Monte a job as a janitor. This is part of the re-entry plan. Get him this job and between me and my tribe, we will ensure he makes it to work on time each day. Each of us takes a day. Things go smoothly for several weeks and then they don't.

Monte calls me and says, Trisse they're going to let me go.

What? I can't believe it. These are friends. They haven't spoken to me. I call the executive director. She tells me Monte isn't cut out for the job. I explain how we likely have to adjust his dosage. This is what working with people who have a mental illness is like. She's not moved and sure enough, she lets Monte go. Monte is broken. He curls up on the couch in my mother's house for months and months and goes inside himself as my mother struggles to support him and Chase, and to a large degree Bernard, whose work is spotty.

And it's Jasmine and Alton, who have relocated to Las Vegas, who get her to shift. After a lifetime in Southern California, my pious mother packs up and heads to Sin City.

They run us out of California, Cherice, Alton says. Come on to Vegas. People can live here, he says. Alton has opened a small mechanic shop, Seven Palms Automotive in Las Vegas, and Jasmine lets my mother know there are jobs and whole houses there that can be rented for cheaper than apartments in LA. I accept this, that my mother is leaving, but I cannot help think that the drug war, the war on gangs, has really been no more than a forced migration project. From my neighborhood in LA to the Bay Area to Brooklyn, Black and Brown people have been moved out as young white people build exciting new lives standing on the bones of ours. The drug war as ethnic cleansing.

Monte and Chase relocate with my Mom but it doesn't last long. He tells me over the phone one night how much he hates it in Vegas, how nothing is familiar to him. He says he wants to come home.

Don't do that, Monte, I say. Wherever Mom is, you're home.

I have no friends here, Trisse.

No one's left in Van Nuys, I say. They're all locked up, I say. Or dead, I say.

Monte pauses.

Cynthia is there, he responds.

And with that, we are right back where we started. It is 2012 now and Monte has been home less than a year and already he is in his third residence. Predictably, it's a disaster. And predictably also, I suppose, it is my mother, again, who has to share the hard news.

Monte's off of his medication, she says. He is breaking up everything at Cynthia's house. Right now as we're speaking, she says. Trisse, please get Paul and get over there.

Mark Anthony and I are living about 45 minutes away from Van Nuys, in an artist's village in central LA called St. Elmo's. We rush over to Cynthia's apartment and as we do, we call Paul: Can you get right over? Paul can get there faster than we can. It will be the first time he will see his baby brother like this. I call him to say we are near and Paul tries to answer, but the only thing that comes through is all this noise in the background.

Brother, brother, look at me, Paul is shouting.

Monte is shouting, too, but I cannot make out his words. But then I hear him begin to cry—which may be a good sign. Crying may exhaust him, may stop him.

When we arrive we step into a house that's been destroyed. Furniture is turned over and some of it's been broken. Plates are smashed. In the center of it all, my brother Paul is holding Monte in his arms, holding him like he held all of us when we were small. Paul is wiping the sweat from Monte's bald head and brow.

Monte has calmed down but Cynthia, understandably, has not. He can't stay here, she says desperately.

I know, I say.

I was on one, huh, Trisse, Monte says, looking up at me from his brother's arms. In this moment he looks like a small boy.

I shake my head. You were, I say, without judgment or anger. I look in my brother's eyes. Monte clearly hasn't slept and getting him rest is a huge priority. But first we have to get him out of there. I tell Paul that Mark Anthony and I will take Monte home with us, which we do. And as we get him to at least lay down, we call the team together. Jason, Tanya, my friend Damon. Mom rushes back into town.

And with no success, we all try to convince Monte he

has to go back into the hospital. I'm writing this in sentences, but this unfolded over days. Over several really hard days. My team, my community, my tribe: they stay with us.

There's an afternoon where Mom presses Monte as much as she can. Please baby. You have to go back to the hospital, she begs. But he associates doctors and hospitals with prison and four- and five-point restraints. He won't listen to us.

I'm not going there again, he says, determined.

We push some more but he refuses any pleas, especially from mom and me. He seems embarrassed around us. I think he thinks he is supposed to protect us, not the other way around. But men have been most present at all of his episodes. Even if it's been men in law enforcement who hate him, he is used to male energy. Monte begins spiraling up. He's terrified.

Someone, I don't recall who, gets him to take his Ativan for his anxiety, but it doesn't work. We're likely past the Ativan stage. Instead of calming down, Monte flashes back to his first time in County Jail, when he was beaten and starved, and before we can stop him, he is in the bathroom where he starts drinking from the toilet. A toilet, during part of his time in LA County Jail, was all he had to drink from. Monte is having a complete flashback, a PTSD-induced flashback. And perhaps because it is so horrible, perhaps because in that moment we are all with Monte in a cage in LA County Jail, it's what does it for us, what steels our reserve. We *will* get Monte to the hospital and get him the help he needs. Negotiations have to ratchet up. Mom, Paul, me and Mark Anthony call in all the troops: Tremaine,

our half-brother from another relationship Alton had; Jason
and Damon. Mark Anthony with his training in healing and
acupuncture serves as the negotiator.

Monte, he begins, we have to get you to the hospital.

Nope, Monte responds.

Monte, can I explain why?

Yup.

Because you're having PTSD, brother. We can't let you
drink from the toilet. It's bad for you and you don't deserve
that. Mark Anthony speaks slowly, his voice gentle as a new
mother's embrace.

Monte is quiet.

We can't help you here the way we want to. We love
you. We want you well.

Monte is thinking.

And then, from Monte, a challenge: I'll go to the hospital if you gimme ten pull-ups in a row. Without stopping.

Now, Mark Anthony is tall but he is super skinny. This
is going to be hard as fuck. But he takes a deep breath and
says, Okay, Monte. And they head out to the pull-up bar we
have in the yard. We all follow them and watch as Mark Anthony struggles, one pull-up, two, three pull-ups, four and
finally, finally, without breaking, he hits it: Ten! He drops
down, breathing heavily. Monte won't go back on his word.
A deal is a deal.

And all the Black men gathered there create a gentle
healing circle around my brother Monte and guide him easy
into Tremaine's car.

My mom and I follow them and en route I call a nurse I

know who works at County USC and tell her we're coming. She doesn't work in psychiatric admissions but she is there and waiting to help guide us when our mini-caravan arrives.

It takes Monte 30, maybe 40 minutes to get out of the car. We wait. And slowly, slowly, I see Monte emerge from the car. He is walking gingerly, Paul on one side and Tremaine on the other. He has a towel over his head. They don't let my brother stumble, they don't let him fall. This is the image of Black men that lives in my head. This constructive care. This steady love.

Mark Anthony walks ahead of them and speaks to the security and somehow finagles his way into the back and helps Monte through the intake and into his room, where he gets the doctor to give my brother a shot so he can really and fully sleep for the first time in three or four days.

Mark Anthony, Tremaine and Paul get back in the car and drive back to our bungalow. My mother and I get in my car and begin to talk about how to help Cynthia put her home together. We have navigated this situation with no police involvement. And that night, before I drift off to sleep laying next to Mark Anthony, I think: this is what community control looks like.

This is what the love of Black men looks like.

This is what our Black yesterday once looked like.

And I think: If we are to survive, this is what our future must look like.

9

NO ORDINARY LOVE

Love takes off the masks we fear we cannot live without and know we cannot live within.

JAMES A. BALDWIN

It's Spike Lee who brings Mark Anthony and I to-gether.

I'm a year ahead of him, a senior in high school and I am obsessed with the Spike Lee Joint *Bamboozled*, a razor-sharp satire that tells the story of a Black man, Pierre Delacroix (whose real name is Peerless Dothan). He's a Harvard grad who is continually humiliated and abused by his white boss at a television network. The white boss, who is married to a Black woman, asserts that he's Blacker than Delacroix and repeatedly, he calls him, Delacroix, *Nigga*.

The white boss refuses to allow any of Delacroix's positive story ideas about Black people to go through, opting only for shows that depict us as vulgar caricatures. Delacroix, desperate to get out of his job, tries to get fired by creating a disgusting, racist minstrel show—blackface and all—but it backfires. The network and white boss love it and the show becomes a success. Eventually, Delacroix embraces the success of the show, spins it as just satire and gets behind it. But by the end, and as a result of the extraordinary pain that arises because of the racist horrific, many of the characters in the film are killed, and there is a strong message about how the media has taught us to hate ourselves and how that hate leads to our death.

Those of us who repeatedly watch *Bamboozled*—kids in my senior class—are deeply impacted by it and its messages. We have conversation after conversation about how racism makes us hate ourselves and misdirects our anger toward one another rather than focusing it on where the sources of the problem lie. We talk about how dangerous media and pop culture can be, how complicit they are in shaping how we move in the world.

I want other students beyond our class to join the conversation, and because during junior year at Cleveland students study the "isms"—racism, sexism, homophobia and classism—I think the film is a perfect vehicle for the junior class. Teachers make a classroom and equipment available to me, and I make flyers and the word gets out about the event. The classroom fills up. Of the roughly 200 students who are part of the arts and humanities program I am in at Cleveland, about 10 percent are Black, and, along with one or two people who are Latinx, one of whom is

white, I think all of them show up. Mark Anthony is among
them.

We have a talkback when the film ends, but the room is
mostly silent. We are too young, we take ourselves too seriously to appreciate the satire. We can only absorb the pain.
Most slowly file out but not Mark Anthony. He's in a chair
in the corner. We haven't really talked before this. But his
head is in his arms. He is not okay. I go over to him, sit atop
the desk beside him, and start speaking gently.

Mark Anthony, I begin, resting my hand on his back.
Are you okay? Do you want to talk?

He is crying and I lean in. I hold him, this beautiful-
looking young man with the wild hair, all long and lean,
and with sparkling green eyes. Slowly, everyone clears the
room to provide us privacy. I move closer and put my arms
around Mark Anthony. He does not want to speak and so
we don't. I just stay with him, hold him, hold space for all
he is feeling but cannot say. We sit like that in our first real
moment together, a moment of utter and complete intimacy.
It feels entirely natural. But vaguely, I'm also aware of something bizarre happening inside of me. I feel . . . attracted
to him?

I don't get it. I have never been attracted to a cisgender (a person whose gender identity matches the sex they
were assigned at birth), heterosexual man. Never. I had come
out two years before and now, at 18, young and fierce in my
sexuality, I am a purist. My attraction is and has been clearly
and specifically to women who at this time are called Studs,
people who will eventually be called gender non-conforming.

The people I am attracted to are masculine of center, to be sure, but not born body, as well as mind and soul, male. I have no idea what to do with these feelings for Mark Anthony. I do know that in my heart, the heart dedicated to Black liberation, I love people. Period. I love complicated, imperfect, beautiful people. People, I suppose, like me.

But in the immediate, I don't have to navigate this strange, unexpected imposition of feelings in my heart, my body. Mark Anthony and I, after this day, develop a friendship that is not rooted in sex. It helps that I am still dating Cheyenne, although we are beginning to grow apart as we grow older and she stops attending Cleveland—mostly because she doesn't have the support she needs to make the long trek to the school from the neighborhood she lives in. But it also helps that sexually, Mark Anthony is very reserved and, at this juncture in his life, has not yet kissed a girl. The chemistry between us is undeniable, but we choose not to translate it sexually. We are just determined to love one another, to share an abiding and deep love with one another. Without sex. We begin spending every day together.

And, as with my other friends, we dive into reading books together. bell hooks continues to be a North Star but Cornel West's work, as well, takes center stage. And, as with other intimate relationships I have had with both friends and lovers, we begin to share a journal, a quiet and private place where we are able to say in poems and paragraphs what we often cannot say in person. Mark Anthony shares in our journal that except for that day in the classroom, after we watched *Bamboozled*, he has never cried in public before, at least not since he was a very small boy. And he doesn't have a particular memory of doing it then, either.

After high school graduation, when Carla and I move in with Donna, for those first heady summer weeks Mark Anthony and I grow closer, speaking every day, seeing one another regularly. We have the innate sense that we can change the world, that everything that is hard and cruel doesn't have to stay that way. Cleveland has provided us tools, and once I become engaged with the Strategy Center, my belief in what is possible expands exponentially. With Mark Anthony, I am finding ways to heal my relationships with Black men, who, for all my love for them, are people who disappear, people who are inconsistent. Because, for all the understanding I now have around prisons and race, I am still just a kid whose fathers, both of them, disappeared. Whose brother did.

I do not, in fact, have an analysis at this time around Alton being gone, about the impact it had on him to have lost his livelihood and ability to care for his family, and I do not have a full analysis at this point even around Gabriel. There is, at this point, very much the feeling, albeit one I do not share often, that he chose drugs over me. The war on drugs has done an incredible job of demonizing the people we need and love the most, of making someone's use of drugs solely a matter of personal responsibility and weakness.

There is rarely discussion about the trauma that often drives chaotic drug use and addiction. And there is no discussion about the fact that fully 75 percent of the people who use drugs never develop addiction. (For some drugs, like marijuana, fully 90 percent of those who use never become addicted.) They wake up, go to work or school, pay their taxes, raise their kids, make love with their partners. They live. They live regular old boring lives. But for my father, my brother, others I know, chaos was a factor before drugs were a part of their lives. Why does no one ever address that?

Where we could see that other laws were race-based and aimed at disrupting Black life, we had—we still have—a hard time accepting drug policy as race policy and the war on drugs as the legal response to the gains of the Civil Rights and Black Power Movements. At the time the drug war was launched, Black people stood, worldwide, atop a moral mountain. America—the world—knew it owed us for centuries of slavery and Jim Crow. And instead of doubling down on how to repair the harm, it made *us* the harm. After removing a debilitating number of jobs and the funding to ensure quality schools, after instituting laws that disrupted families' possibility to thrive—welfare laws beginning in the 1970s meant that women often lost benefits needed to feed their children if they had a man present in the home, even if between the two of them they still subsisted on poverty wages—our mothers and fathers and daughters and sons were criminalized for choices made often out of absolute desperation and lack of any other real options.

Consider: In the wake of Katrina, there were two Getty images that Yahoo News ran two days after the storm hit. In the first photo, two white residents waded through the water with food. Beneath their picture, the caption read: "Two residents wade through chest-deep water after finding bread and soda from a local grocery store after Hurricane Katrina came through the area in New Orleans, Louisiana." Right after it, they ran an image of a Black boy also wading through the water with food. The caption read, "A young man walks through chest-deep flood water after looting a grocery store in New Orleans on Tuesday, Aug. 30, 2005."

This is what it is like every day. Harm to white people, especially resourced white people, and the behaviors they engage in as a result, is framed sympathetically. Harm to us, more widespread, more embedded, more permanent, is framed as our own doing.

This is to say that for a long time and for all the structural analysis I was learning about race and the world, at the end of the day, I was still just a teenager with a heart left broken.

But then one day that summer, I don't hear from Mark Anthony. We had been in the habit of talking not once but throughout the day, the days. I call him and call him but there's no answer. This is before the age of texting and many of us do not have cell phones. So I call a landline that rings until it rings out. Mark Anthony is totally a ghost. This goes on for probably two weeks, this painful silence. It feels like longer.

Finally, I write a long letter, a letter Mark Anthony will later call my hate letter. I write it in red pen. I give it to John Ralph, Mark Anthony's brother, who is a friend and whom I still see when we all hang out at our friend Tanya's house—without Mark Anthony.

Two days later the landline at Donna's rings. And

although at first I don't recognize the voice, I realize suddenly: it's Mark Anthony! I am both joyous and enraged. But we have protocols among our little tribe. We are committed to courageous conversations. Our school had taught us to address conflict in ways young people are not typically provided; as often as possible, we, as a group, use them. I want to do that here. Not long before, Cheyenne and I had a torturous breakup—she'd left me for one of my friends. I don't want to end anything in such a harsh way again. We agree to meet at Tanya's house. It's more than neutral territory. It's sort of our safe house, what with her liberal mother and artistic family.

When I arrive I look different than the last time Mark Anthony saw me. I have shaved my head and gotten a piercing beneath my bottom lip. I've gotten a tattoo on my lower back of a woman flexing her biceps, inspired by Rosie the Riveter. I'm leaning all the way into my feminism and physically demonstrating it in every way I can and tattoos and piercings represent a public commitment to me.

Mark Anthony is as gorgeous as ever. He's grown his hair out into a huge Afro, making him appear even taller than his six feet. When he sees me, he looks me over approvingly, and immediately we are playful, giggling for no reason, touching each other in ways as silly as they are loving. And in the middle of the silliness, the words about nothing, the laughter, Mark Anthony turns serious.

I'm sorry, he says. I will never do that again, he says.

His words break open the container of feelings we've held for the last few weeks.

I talk about my fears, rooted in real-world experience, with cisgender men.

Y'all are not emotionally available, I accuse.

We were getting so intimate, he confesses. I felt too vulnerable, he continues. I felt you could see parts of me others could not. Parts I wasn't ready for the world to see. I didn't feel in control, he says. I don't want people to know how things hurt me, where they hurt me, he explains.

We talk about Black men and the performance of cool, about how brothers are supposed to take whatever the world throws at them and never be fazed. Never be shaken or afraid. I demanded, our relationship demanded, honesty, which is to say vulnerability. Before me, Mark Anthony had never cried in the presence of a peer. Maybe as a child, with his family, but not all naked and out in the world like this.

Mark Anthony apologizes to me again. He tells me, he promises me, he will never, ever disappear on me again. And after this, we begin to date, although we are still nonsexual, and frankly, we are not monogamous. What we are is inexorably bound to one another, to a love and a relationship that we understand and that makes complete sense to us, although it's also true that it engenders discomfort in the others we date. But our position to those people is simple: we are connected. Unbreakable.

The people we date have to accept who we are to each other. One of the writers we studied together and loved was the feminist anarchist Emma Goldman. She offered these words in 1897, at the turn of a new century: "I demand the independence of woman, her right to support herself; to live for herself; to love whomever she pleases, or as many as she pleases. I demand freedom for both sexes, freedom of action, freedom in love and freedom in motherhood."

Goldman, a Russian-born woman who emigrated to America, would be identified by German sexologist Magnus Hirschfeld as "the first and only woman, indeed the first and only American, to take up the defense of homosexual love before the general public." Indeed, she writes to Hirschfeld not only about homosexuality, but also about gender identity existing along a spectrum.

From Goldman we take the lesson that relationships do not come before community liberation, that possessiveness and jealousy can undo the best of us. We strive to be different, to love and honor the singular us along with the collective us. We want to build a world in which undeveloped and unrefined emotional instincts—like possessiveness and jealousy—are minimized as much as humanly possible so that all eyes, hearts and spirits are not distracted from the goal. And the goal is freedom. The goal is to live beyond fear. The goal is to end the occupation of our bodies and souls by the agents of a larger American culture that demonstrates daily how we don't matter.

They show us this in the schools most Black people attend where there are history books—*history books*—sometimes more than a generation old.

They show us every time we drive through one of our neighborhoods that has no safe places for kids or grocery stores.

They show us when they find money for another war but not for a decent hospital we can go to.

They show us on TV and in the movies.

They show us when we are arrested for standing together in the street.

They show us relentlessly.

Which is why we are determined to show ourselves something else. We are determined to love ourselves the best and most whole way we know. For Mark Anthony and I this mostly means being platonic, it means being radically honest about what we feel, even when what we feel seems scary or uncomfortable but also totally natural. Another way of saying that is that in 2003, four years after we first met, Mark Anthony and I kiss for the first time.

We'd spent an evening at a Talib Kweli concert:

WE WORK 'TIL WE BREAK OUR BACK AND YOU HEAR

THE CRACK OF THE BONE

TO GET BY . . . JUST TO GET BY . . .

WE COMMUTE TO COMPUTERS

SPIRITS STAY MUTE WHILE YOU EAGLES SPREAD RUMORS

WE SURVIVALISTS, TURNED TO CONSUMERS

TO GET BY . . . JUST TO GET BY

The night was magical and we cannot stop thinking about each other all through the next day and, by the evening we are on the phone until finally Mark Anthony says, I'm coming to scoop you. And he does. We go back to his apartment, where we listen to the soundtrack from the film *Amandla*. We imagine freedom. Our community's freedom. Our own personal freedom.

We do not make love but we are love. We kiss all night. Another man might have tried to push harder. But Mark Anthony just flows with me and I flow with him. It is perfect, a dream. And we can no longer deny it. We are in love. For six months we flow like this, connected, individual but as one. And then one day he disconnects. He is vacant. He is distant. I push. I ask what's wrong. He just shakes his head. He is gone. I flash back to the summer after high school and my heart wrenches. This time I do not ask why, what happened. I just accept it. He broke a promise and that breaks us. We stay in touch but as a couple, we are over.

And honestly, while it's painful, it's not as hard as it was the first time. This time I am more sure of myself, and before long I am headlong in another relationship with Starr, the rapper and singer. Starr is a Stud and I feel like I am back home. I lose myself in them, in their artistry, our passion, for five years. But those years are punctured by as much intense sensuality as they are by anger. It is the first and only relationship I've ever had where we yell more than we laugh. Even still we try, we push, we *want* us to work. We consider marrying. But the volatility serves neither of us. All my skills around how to have courageous confrontation go to shit. I'm sad and shaken. I miss the healing light that surrounded Mark Anthony and I; Mark Anthony who I never yelled with.

We, Mark Anthony and I, begin to see more of each

other. Again. Apart, we have also grown ever more together. Both of us live in the tradition of Ifa, the African
spiritual practice that originated with the Yoruba people
of Nigeria at least 8,000 years ago. The tradition is earth-
centered and is balanced by these three: Olodumare, Orisha
and Ancestors. Our Supreme Being is known as Olodumare
and is without gender. Olodumare is benevolent, not the
vengeful, angry God I grew up with. Olodumare does not
interfere with the affairs of humans. Rather, Olodumare has
provided us with a Universe, with all that is needed to create
joy and peace—if we so choose it.

In Ifa we believe that all living beings, all elements of
Nature, are interdependent and possessing of soul. Rocks.
Flowers. Rivers. Clouds. Thunder. The Wind. These ener-
gies are called Orisha and it is these Orisha with whom we
are in direct contact, whether we know it or not.

In Ifa, we also recognize and believe that our Ancestors
are always with us and must be honored and acknowledged.
They are part of what both grounds and guides us, and to
understand them, we undertake a process of Divination,
readings that help us understand that our purpose and
destiny are based on the wisdom of the Orishas and the
Ancestors.

Separately Mark Anthony and I both get the same reading: we are meant to be together. I get a reading that says it
outright: Mark Anthony is meant to be your husband.

I ignore the Divination at first. I feel like a fraud and
I tell Mark Anthony this. How is it that I, a Queer woman,
can be destined to be with Mark Anthony? It makes no

sense. Plus, it is hard to ignore or miss the heteronormativity and patriarchy that is threaded through Ifa, compliments of some of its practitioners. But again and again we are told we are each other's soulmates.

He comes over and we process.

The last eight years, he says. We always knew it would come to this.

He's right.

I tell Starr that neither of us is getting what we deserve in our relationship, that I can no longer be here.

I'll change, Starr says. I promise, they say.

It would have happened already, I say.

How dare you leave me for some fucking dude, they say.

I'm not leaving you for some dude, I say. I am leaving because we're not healthy, I say. And Mark Anthony is not some dude, I do not say. Plus I'm already struggling with so much internally. I never thought, never could have imagined I'd want to marry a cis man. But there can be a universe of difference between what you think and what you feel. And I feel Mark Anthony, all the way to the core of me, in the very seat of my heart.

It's a particularly unpleasant breakup with Starr, marked by months of angry texts and notes left on my car. And because we are in a primarily Queer community, we have few resources for how to handle what really becomes abusive. There are community, non-police-involved interventions for challenges in heteronormative and white intimate partner mistreatment, but not really any for us. I think about the numbers of Black women who suffer abuse at the hands of their husbands and lovers because calling the cops is a worse option than getting your ass kicked. In the Black/people of color Queer community, it's even worse.

It takes months of abusive behavior before I am able to block Starr all the way from my life, which also teaches me something about how much I tolerate in the name of transformation. The price is unfair. I want to be at peace, in peace. I pull Mark Anthony closer and he pulls me closer. He agrees to grow with me, to be vulnerable and emotionally available. Mark Anthony moves in with me almost immediately and then we are offered the cabin in Topanga Canyon and we move there, our first home together. The home where I hear the news that my father has died.

It is Mark Anthony who carries me through that loss. Mark Anthony who facilitates a full yearlong healing group with my friends where we come together and make art projects, collages, tiles, paintings to commemorate Gabriel. They come for me but they also come for Gabriel and to process their own grief. When he was with us, when he was alive, Gabriel had been a community dad, and my friends came to Brignac family barbecues, Brignac family baseball. Sometimes two of us make it, sometimes ten. Sometimes we are in our home and sometimes we are at the ocean. But for a solid year, they hold me up, every single week. All facilitated by Mark Anthony. The man Ifa said was to be my husband.

On a brilliant sunny day, September 11, 2010, in a house we rent near the port in San Pedro, a house that had been

fashioned as a traditional Louisiana home, a house that
brought my father into the space, and before more than 200
people, Cullors and Brignacs, all of Mark Anthony's family,
all of the family we created together, we commit ourselves
to each other and we commit ourselves to our community.
We do not marry in the eyes of the law since, at the time,
not everyone could marry in the eyes of the law, but our
commitment is just as deep.

Alton and my father's little brother, Ellis, walk me down
the aisle and Mark's mama walks him down the aisle. He
looks exquisite in his modified white zoot suit—our wedding is 40s style. And I feel as beautiful as ever in my two-
piece, white, crop-topped, form-fitted dress my auntie made
me, the pearls my grandma loaned me to wear. My homegirl
sings Sade—"No Ordinary Love." And we exchange rings
made of wood. And when we jump the broom, all of our 15
friends who stand up with us jump the broom, too. And then
we dance until we can't dance anymore.

Uncle Ellis grabs me by the arm and says, I don't know
what just happened and I've never been to nothing like this
but it was the dopest shit I ever been a part of!

And my mother just says she is proud. She says she is
happy.

Mark Anthony and I and our friends all go to our favorite diner together, Swingers in Santa Monica, and we laugh
more and all fall in love more and then he and I head over
to the W Hotel in Westwood where we've booked a suite
for the night and we hold one another and we wrap ourselves in one another. We have this 24 hours before I have

to be back at UCLA and Mark Anthony back in studies of Chinese medicine. And we whisper to each other how much we love each other, we say I love you 1,000 times. And we say we have hope and we say we have faith. And then slowly we give in to our magnificent, beautifully earned love informed by two souls that are exhausted but sated and certain in the knowledge that yes, while there is so much hell on this earth, so much pain, there is also this. A love we could not have predicted but always imagined. A love that rocks us and a love that holds us. A love not ordinary.

10

DIGNITY AND POWER.
NOW.

Every defeat, every heartbreak, every loss, contains its own
seed, its own lesson on how to improve.

MALCOLM X

Monte has always been the sibling who is closest to
me. He is the one I play with the most, joke with the most.
Our relationship has nearly its own language. Not in the way
we think of when we think of twins. But me and Monte,
we never need full sentences, wholly spoken thoughts, to
communicate fully with one another. In every way, he is my
first best friend. Losing him at such a young age is an early
childhood wound it will take me more than a decade to
really unpack, understand and begin to try to heal. I am 11
when the police start picking up Monte, who is then 14, and
putting him in juvie, for hanging out in the street, for underage drinking, for tagging—which gets him put on the

National Gang Database. And I am still a teenager when he is tortured by the Los Angeles County Sheriff's Department.

There's a difference between abuse and torture. Both are horrible, often unbearable, and both leave scars. Neither can be minimized. But I make the distinction here in order to explain that while abuse may or may not be intentional, and is often spontaneous, torture is *always* intentional. It is *always* premeditated. It is planned out and its purpose is to deliberately and systematically dismantle a person's identity and humanity. It is designed to destroy a sense of community and eliminate leaders and create a climate of fear. This is the definition used by the Center of Victims of Torture.

In a sentence, torture is terrorism.

And this is what my brother endures.

He is not alone.

Because while I know the basics of what he experienced the first time he was sent to LA County Jail in 1999, a jail run by the sheriff's department, it will not be until 2011 when I read a report issued by the ACLU of Southern California that I fully understand what was done to my brother there. This is to say that Abu Ghraib was first practiced on this soil, in this America. And before the attack on the World Trade Center and the Pentagon. Before the second Gulf War. The skills to torture people were honed in this nation on people who were not terrorists. They were the victims of terrorism.

In the fall of 2011, weeks after Monte's come home from Corcoran State Prison, and days after he's back in my mother's house from the hospital stay, I'm in our cottage in the Village with Mark Anthony and our friend Ray. And on this night I'm going through my email when I notice one from the ACLU of Southern California. They have filed an 86-page complaint against the LA County Sheriff's department for *torture*. Seventy of the 86 pages are testimonies from survivors and those who were witnesses to torture. The report, which includes prisoners' testimony and that of jailhouse chaplains who could not be silent, reveals that under the watch of Sheriff Lee Baca, torture in the LA County Jail was, for at least two decades, pervasive, gruesome, systemic and routine.

The scope of the report is staggering.

The sheer number of individuals who were kicked in the testicles, set upon and beaten by several deputies at once, individuals who were tased for no apparent reason other than the entertainment of guards, who had bones broken by guards wielding flashlights and other everyday tools that became instruments of extreme violence in America's largest jail, is breathtaking enough. But other elements of the torture almost break me as I read the words of a civilian who testified about a wheelchair-bound prisoner whom deputies pulled off his bed, kicked and kneed in his ribs, back and neck and then shot with pepper spray in his face. I begin to hyperventilate and remember my brother on his knees drinking out of the toilet. My God.

I can't breathe.

We can't breathe.

Mr. "GGG" testifies about the deputy who forcibly searched a prisoner's buttocks with a flashlight, placing the flashlight half an inch into the prisoner's rectum, which caused extensive enough injury that the man bled and bled. But he didn't complain because the last prisoner who did was taken away and attacked by several other guards, the screams, a haunting that refuses to be calmed or set aside. It returns and returns.

Aaaaaaaahhhhhh!!!!!!!!

Noooooooooooooooo!!!!!!!

PLLLLLLLLLEEEEEAAAAASSSSE!!!!

Fingers, hands, collarbones, jaws and ribs were broken.

Eyes were popped out of sockets.

Arms and shoulders were regularly dislocated.

Prisoners who were already rendered unconscious continued to be assaulted. In most every case the prisoner was reported by independent observers as not resisting. Many were handcuffed from the moment the attack was initiated.

One man was stripped naked and locked in a cell with other prisoners who were encouraged to rape him, which they did.

Male guards participated in torture. Female guards participated in torture. Everyone knew what was happening. Medical staff knew what was happening. The sheriff knew what was happening.

And it is reading this that makes me finally understand, in a way I had not before, what had been done to my brother. My Monte. My best friend. Stripped. Beaten.

Starved. Forced to drink water from a toilet. What else. And what fucking else?

Monte's testimony is not in those pages, those stories of survivors. But my brother is a survivor. My whole family is. I begin to flashback and suddenly it is 1999 and I am watching my mother desperately trying to find my brother. My mother is calling and calling. No one is helping her. I am a kid. I want someone to help my mother. I want someone to help my brother. I want someone to help me. But no one does. No one.

Please, I can hear my mother say as though it's happening again, Please, I am looking for my son. His name is Monte Cullors, she says to anyone who will listen, but no one will listen.

In my cottage in the Village in 2011 I begin to cry as Mark Anthony and Ray circle around me in support. What is happening? they want to know.

I shake my head in overwhelm and point to the screen and then I reach for the phone and call my mother.

Mom? Mom? Are you there with Monte? I ask.

Yes, she says.

Can he hear me too? And she must have signaled him to pick up another extension.

They're suing the LA County Jail, I say. For torturing prisoners, I say.

My mother and Monte are silent.

And then after several seconds, maybe as long as half a minute, my mom says, Thank God.

And then after an even longer pause, Monte says, slowly and ever so quietly but ever so resolutely, Finally.

Immediately I know I want to tell the world what has happened, and I say to Mark Anthony and Ray, I have to do an art piece. And almost as immediately, I go to work.

I pull together four friends who are exquisite performers, blow up pages of the complaint to 8 by 11 feet. I call my mother and ask:

Do you have the documentation of the phone calls you made to the jail?

I sure do, she says. I kept everything, she says.

I get the documentation and audiotape her written record and I get the audio of the sheriff and under-sheriff being questioned by the commission that is pulled together after the report is released. I buy caution tape, and then approach a local art space that has often allowed us to do political performance work. I call the work *Stained,* and when audiences walk in, they see on the walls testimonies:

1. Deputies beat Mr. KK so violently that he suffered a fractured jaw, and required eye surgery and stitches in his ear. The incident began after deputies searched all the cells on Mr. KK's row, and Mr. KK noticed that some of his property was missing, including items he had just purchased from the commissary. After asking to speak with a sergeant about the missing property, Mr. KK reported that a deputy shoved him hard against

a wall, slapped his ear, punched his face several times, and threw him to the ground. With Mr. KK on the ground, the deputy kicked him roughly ten times in the face, jaw, and back of his head, causing a large pool of Mr. KK's blood to form on the floor. The deputy then kicked Mr. KK's ear three times, an experience Mr. KK described as more painful than when he was hit by a car.

2. A Men's Central Jail deputy attacked inmate Mr. JJ after Mr. JJ had said the deputy "didn't have a date since high school." The deputy slammed Mr. JJ to the ground, and, with another deputy, searched Mr. JJ's property and threw his belongings in the toilet. The deputy stomped on Mr. JJ's hand with his boot, shattering his knuckle, and the deputies kicked Mr. JJ's body. The deputies used a Taser on Mr. JJ, who suffers from epilepsy, and shot pepper spray into his face. Mr. JJ suffered extensive bruises, and required surgery on the shattered knuckle in his hand.

3. Deputies punched inmate Juan Pablo Reyes over and over again in the ribs, back, mouth, and eyes, breaking his eye socket and leaving his body badly bruised. When Reyes fell to the ground, deputies kicked him with their steel-toed boots, ignoring his cries. They did not stop there. The deputies ordered him to strip. They then forced him to walk naked up and down the hallway of a housing module, in full view of other inmates. One deputy yelled "Gay boy walking." As he walked, Reyes

cried. The deputies laughed. They then placed him in a
cell with inmates who beat and sexually assaulted him.
The deputies ignored Mr. Reyes's repeated pleas to be
taken out of the cell.

Caution tape separates the audience members from the
four performers who are each standing alone, as if in solitary confinement. They wear white t-shirts, grey sweats and
black Converse sneakers and each uses their body in a different way to demonstrate the impact of being caged.

One brother does burpees until he collapses.

One woman laughs until she starts crying and then starts
laughing again and she loops like that for the entire show.

One person paces in circles and refuses to stop.

The final performer jumps and jumps, trying desperately to reach a sky they cannot see.

The audience hears the audio recorded for the performance: They hear the dates and notes my mother kept and
took of the dozens of calls she made in search of her son.
They hear the dates and notes about the dozens of times
she was rebuffed. They hear the time she finally gets through
to the jail psychiatrist she was referred to by the watch
commander. The psychiatrist takes the call but tells my
mother nothing about Monte, who at this point we do not
know has been diagnosed as having schizoaffective disorder. Instead, the psychiatrist takes the time to admonish
my mother: You're rude, she says, to have called here so
many times! What's wrong with you?

The audience hears the questioning of the sheriff and

under-sheriff by the commission: What kind of jail were you running, Sheriff Baca, that allowed deputies to feel so safe in their behavior that they often beat prisoners in full view of civilians, including ACLU lawyers and representatives and chaplains?

The show will tour for two years, but by the second show my homegirl from the Strategy Center, Francesca, will say to me, You have to do more. You can do more. She nurtures me and my growth and my vision with the love and support of a midwife. And I want not one more person to know what Monte or any of the prisoners in that report knew. I want no family to ever feel what we've felt. As the program tours, we begin to envision and create the infrastructure for a campaign: The Coalition to End Sheriff Violence. Launched in September 2012, our initial goal is to establish and ensure civilian oversight of the sheriff's department.

But as the organizing work grows, Mark Anthony and I know we need a fully realized organization in order to support it. And I am scared to do this, of course. But I also know I am not 17-year-old Patrisse who first came to the Strategy Center, the one organization I have been a part of for all of these years, the organization that I've volunteered for, at that point, all of my adult life. And while I am committed to always remaining a member of the Center, I know it is time to leave my proverbial home, and take into the world all the lessons it has given me, including how to launch, execute and win campaigns by building power among those the world considers powerless.

We had stopped the fines associated with truancy in Los

Angeles despite having to do it with parents and students who were both poor and criminalized and publicly shamed. If we could do that, then we could stop the sheriff's office with moms and dads and sisters, brothers, cousins and friends whose loved ones had been disappeared. Whose loved ones had been beaten. Whose loved ones had been tortured.

We call our organization Dignity and Power Now.

And in 2016 we establish the first civilian oversight board of the LA County Sheriff's Department.

11

BLACK LIVES MATTER

This was a teenager just trying to get home.

SYBRINA FULTON

It is July 13, 2013, and I have stepped away from monitoring events at the trial of the man who killed Trayvon Martin, 17, a year and a half before.

I had learned about Trayvon one day while I was at the Strategy Center in 2012 and going through Facebook. I came across a small article from a local paper. Was it Sanford's? I read that a white man—that's how the killer was identified and self-identified until we raised the issue of race—had killed a Black boy and was not going to be charged.

I start cursing. I am outraged. In what fucking world does this make sense? I put a call out: Have people heard about 17-year-old Trayvon Martin? I have loved so many young men who look just like this boy. I feel immediate grief, and as my friends begin to respond, they, too, are grief stricken. We meet at my home. We circle up. A multiracial group of roughly 15 people dedicated to ending white supremacy and creating a world in which all of our children can thrive. We process. We talk about what we've seen and experienced in our lives. We cry.

At some point Al Sharpton hears about what happened to Trayvon and a huge rally is held in New York. An arrest is demanded. And at first it seems ignored. But the demand is elevated in Florida by a group of brilliant and brave young organizers, the Dream Defenders, led by Umi Agnew. They occupy the governor's office, bringing direct action back into the fore for our generation. They use social media to amplify their voices, and they inspire a nation of organizers, including me, as I am working in LA to build out Dignity and Power Now. After weeks of protest, the killer is arrested and the world begins to know the extent to which he is a sick and deranged man, a man whose violence was known, a man who had had police called on him. A man who was not called a terrorist or put on a national database despite, before he murdered Trayvon, having committed actual violence.

Before the killer's trial begins, there are several things that we know:

In July 2005, he was arrested for "resisting an officer with violence." According to Jonathan Capehart, reporting for *The Washington Post*, the man who was allowed to carry a gun and become a neighborhood watch volunteer "got into a scuffle with cops who were questioning a friend for alleged underage drinking." The *Post* continued: "The charges were reduced and then waived after he entered an alcohol education program."

In August 2005, the killer's fiancée sought and received a restraining order against him because of his alleged violence against her.

Over an eight-year period, the killer made more than 45 unsubstantiated calls to the Sanford, Florida, police department about people he termed as "suspicious black males."

The killer's cousin had accused him of molesting her *before* the case made national news—meaning before any attention-seeking could have been her motive—and reported to the police, "I know George. And I know that he does not like black people." She pleaded for anonymity, and she continued: "He would start something. He's a very confrontational person. It's in his blood. Let's just say that. I don't want this poor kid and his family to just be overlooked." She begged police to ask around, to find out what kind of man this was.

All of this was in the record before Reverend Sharpton's rally.

Before the demand that he be arrested. Before the Dream Defenders occupied the governor's office.

Before Black Lives Matter.

But on July 13, 2013, I am traveling to Susanville, California, to visit an 18-year-old young man named Richie whom I have known and cherished since he was 14 years old. Richie has been sentenced to a decade in prison for a rob-

bery in which no one was physically harmed. What kind of
time will Trayvon's killer get?

We have driven fully half a day to be here, to be with
Richie, whom I met when Mark Anthony, Jason and I
worked as youth counselors at Cleveland. We initiated various forms of restorative justice programming in the school,
and Richie stood out, even among a cohort of young people
who were all standouts. He was part of a group of Black boys
at the high school who couldn't stay out of trouble—we
were told. But we believed punishment was the wrong in-
terrupter for them.

Suspensions, for example, did little to move young
people to wholeness or better performance. And they were
used for even the most minor of offenses—being "disre-
spectful" was a common cause. Black children were far
more at risk, suspended at nearly four times the rate of white
students despite similar behavior patterns. Black children
taught by white teachers were particularly at risk for suspension, the data showed again and again. (Although the reverse was not true. Black teachers did not move to suspend
white children at higher rates.)

Nearly seven million kids in the nation, some as young
as four, were suspended in 2011 and 2012, when we were
at Cleveland. Still, suspensions, for as widely as they were
used, were a failure. All they did, as the data indicated, was
alienate young people from school, teachers and often their
peers. And they, like other punitive measures, did not address the external life and social factors that impacted

children, including food and housing insecurity and police
harassment or having lost a parent or close family member
to mass incarceration.

But our job, in any case, was to interrupt that trouble
and we were determined to do it in a way that elevated the
humanity of the students. For a year our small team sat
in circle with the young men. We talked about racism and
homophobia. We talked about classism and sexism. We
pulled apart concepts of addiction, and not so much addiction as in drugs but as in all of the behaviors that can com-
pel a person to behave in ways that are detrimental. Our
vision was to interrupt the process that had led the young
men to see themselves outside of their own dreams.

Richie was the intellectual and the artist in the crew. He
was the first one to publicly declare that he was a feminist, to
say he wanted to be a Black man unlike his father, whose
definition of manhood was prescribed by a limited Judeo-
Christian ethos: make money, marry, have a child, rule your
home, die. Richie eventually became the editor of the school
newspaper and for the Valentine's Day edition one year, he
supported a young woman writer who, like many of the students, had been reading Eve Ensler and wanted to proclaim
V-Day as a day to celebrate and honor vaginas.

She wrote about how sacred they were, about how they
must no longer be the site of male assault. Richie commis-
sioned art to accompany the story and when the paper
came out, he made it front-page news, along with a huge
picture of a vulva. The school administration went wild,
confiscating all the copies of the paper, threatening Richie

with suspension. He stood his ground. He said it was their responsibility to talk about sexual assault, their duty to force people to think about women's sexual organs differently. He said women were powerful and ought to be honored as such.

His position would garner global attention. Richie was called for interviews from as far away as India. Eventually the school backed down from their censure of and threats against him. The experience changed him and by the time he was 18, he had moved out of his parents' home, wanting desperately to break away from the silence of his mother and the harsh boundaries of his father. And after staying with me and Mark Anthony for a time, and then with other friends, he found a small apartment in Reseda, not far from Cleveland, and got a job with the LA Unified School District, working with students not so different than the student he had once been. Life was going well.

Until one day it wasn't.

Without warning, the district cut his hours. And that was that. They didn't fire him, but they didn't give him a steady schedule or allow him to earn a living wage. And because his schedule was erratic, it was hard for him to find anything else. Richie, a six-foot-five, young Black man who was living on his own and who had tattoos, and who was good enough to be hired but not good enough to really include and provide a career path for—and yet not bad enough to fire, was left in limbo and desperate. And his rent was due.

Later, after he was arrested, he said to me that when he felt desperate, when he didn't have the money to pay his rent, the voice he heard in his head was the one he was raised with: Men don't ask for help. Men make it happen.

You had already done so much for me, he said to me in the LA County Jail visitor's room. I didn't want to appear weak, he said. I know that's stupid, he said, but it's how I felt.

I told him he could always ask me for help. He said, I don't know what I was thinking. I guess I figured if I didn't hurt anyone, if I just got the money, it would get me through and no one would have to know, he said. I know that sounds crazy. I didn't want to hurt anyone. I just needed to pay the rent.

And in fact no one was physically hurt, although I'm sure they were terrified. But Richie was still handed down a sentence of ten years. Like Monte, who also never hurt anyone, was handed a sentence of eight years. When I think about them as I write these words, I don't only think about all the killer cops, the cops who lied, the cops who never got charged or when they were got acquitted. I also think about men like Brock Turner, the Stanford star swimmer, who raped a woman and got six months. Six months because the judge said Turner couldn't make it in prison, that prison wasn't for him.

But it was made for Richie? For Monte? For my father? My God. Is that not reason enough to shut it down?

But on this hot July day in 2013, Richie is thick in the first year of that sentence and we, his wife, Taina, his best friend Haewon and I, are sitting in a prison visiting room in Susanville that is like most California prison visiting rooms, sterile and windowless, with tables that have the legs cut down to three inches off the ground, so no playing footsies. There are the requisite vending machines against a wall where we can buy overpriced food that ensures lucrative contracts for white-owned companies and salty, sugary, processed food items that are loaded guns for we who have no real choice but to eat them.

And on this day in Susanville we are talking about a million things, although eventually everything will come back to what is unfolding in Central Florida and Trayvon Martin's killer: Will he walk?

For as much as we are there in California for and with Richie, together, loving each other and laughing as much as is possible, we are also in Florida and our hearts are full with the Fulton and Martin family and we are afraid. We do not speak of our fear about the decision that looms, knowing that our children so rarely receive justice in this nation. We speak about hope because after all, what else? At some point I recall thinking, My God. The world knows that, against a 911 operator's orders, this man chased down and killed 17-year-old Trayvon Martin.

And Trayvon Martin, a Black boy who was just walking home. Walking with a can of Arizona Iced Tea and a pack of Skittles he'd bought for his little brother. Walking and speaking on his cell to his friend Rachel, a girl who was bullied and a girl he protected. Walking and wearing a hoodie like teenagers everywhere wear hoodies. Walking and at once set upon by a large, white-presenting man who decided that because the boy was Black and because he wore a hoodie like most teens, he was a threat.

We learn that the man was ordered by a police dispatcher to stop.

We learn that the man chased the boy, who was running errands for his little brother, who was talking to his friend, his friend who was bullied.

We learn that the man pulled the trigger on this unarmed child who weighed what, 50, 75 pounds less than the man with the gun?

We learn that the man believed he had a right to do what he did. A right to stand ground that wasn't being challenged by a boy carrying iced tea and Skittles. He believed that his assumed rights superseded this child's right to walk home to his own house to bring his little brother a treat.

And we are scared that a jury of this man's peers would agree.

We are scared because of the work and time it took even to get the man arrested.

We are scared because Trayvon's beautiful life and terrible death is meant to be erased; the reporting of it made no front-page news, no *Dateline,* no Anderson Cooper. The story on my Facebook feed was a tiny blog post, a post not connected with mainstream media. A white man is questioned and then released after he shoots and kills an unarmed Black boy who was walking home. And in that instant I was filled with rage and confusion. Was this 2012 or 1955?

We could be talking about Emmett Till. This is who I

think about throughout the course of the trial and the weeks and months leading up to it. I think of Emmett Till and his family and also my nephew, Chase, Monte's son, who is 14 the year Trayvon is killed. Will he be shot down and killed for walking while Black, and will his murder matter so little it doesn't even make the news and no one will be held accountable?

I grew up in a neighborhood that was impoverished and in pain and bore all the modern-day outcomes of communities left without resources and yet supplied with tools of violence. But when someone in my neighborhood committed a crime, let alone murder, all of us were held accountable, my God. Metal detectors, searchlights and constant police presence, full-scale sweeps of kids just walking home from school—all justified by politicians and others who said they represented our needs. Where were these representatives when white guys shot us down?

Were it not for the brave and determined young people who formed the Dream Defenders joining forces with the brave and heartbroken parents of Trayvon, Sybrina Fulton and Tracey Martin, and had there not been sit-ins, protests, occupations, and Al Sharpton, this boy's name would be on no one's tongue, save for his family and the friends who loved him.

Because of all this, we know and we are afraid, but still, in that prison in Susanville on July 13, 2013, in the state that would give a desperate Black boy who physically harmed no one ten years but a rapist six months, we hold on to hope.

Because what else?

Seven hours after it begins, the visit with Richie ends, and we head back to the motel we are staying at in the small town. Of the just under 20,000 residents, nearly half, 46 percent, live in one of the town's two prisons.

Susanville, incorporated in 1860, was named for the child of the man who laid claim to founding it at a time when founding something was a euphemism for manifest destiny and homesteading and all the blood and death both of these wrought. "Founding," a term like the phrase "collateral damage," the use of which was ratcheted up in the 90s so they didn't have to say dead Iraqi children.

But the point is that we are an 11-hour drive from Los Angeles because Susanville is deep in Northern California, farther up than the Bay Area and at the border of Nevada, near Reno. And it's entirely unlike the vibrancy and wealth generally associated with our state and its outsize imagery of glittery Beverly Hills and shiny Silicon Valley. If you saw a picture of it, West Virginia would likely come to mind before California would.

But Susanville is actually more reflective of the average California town than anything that is marketed to tourists. And it looks like American towns across the rest of the country: small and working class, except here the demographics report an extraordinary diversity—if, that is, diversity is distorted, like a horror-house mirror or a story from *The Twilight Zone*. In Susanville, there is almost no one who is Black and free at the same time, although a cursory reading of census reports could have you believing it's a racial Kumbaya.

Once a place where loggers and miners worked, today Susanville's singular growth industry is prisons; roughly half of all the adults who live here work at one of the two facilities. Of course those numbers intensify wildly if you count the work done, the labor extracted, from the prisoners who are shipped here predominantly from LA County, from the Bay.

Being here, looking at the storefronts, the people, it feels like we are trapped in a black-and-white photograph from the deep South in the 1950s, and the images of hard rural living come stuttering back as if to taunt us that freedom has never arrived and won't. All you can feel are the walls and the bars, the gun towers and barbed wire, which is only offset by all the military. The random appearance of soldiers who are based near Susanville. The sense of impending war. The American flags in every size you can imagine. What must it be like to live hoping for and invested in war and crime because without them the people of Susanville must believe that the world would collapse?

On the way back to the motel we stop at a small store to buy microwavables. There are no restaurants we want to eat in, plus this is cheaper. We buy pre-made chicken sandwiches or something like that. We are trying to be healthy. The motel has a microwave. We eat and we get on my laptop. Eating and waiting for the verdict to come in. I go on my Facebook page because that's where everyone is updating what's happening. I am nervous but Facebook keeps me connected.

And then it happens.

I start seeing the timelines update. The killer is acquitted of the first charge. And then he is acquitted of all of them. Every. Single. One. Of. Them. I go into shock. I lose my breath. My heart drops to my stomach. I am stunned and for a moment cannot move. When I begin to move I go into denial.

No! This is impossible. Wait a minute. Hold on. This doesn't make sense.

But as soon as I deny it I know that it is true, and I am overcome with embarrassment and shame. How could this have happened? Why couldn't we make this not happen? And then I start crying. And I feel wrong about crying. My tears make me want to hide. I feel like I have to be the particular kind of strong Black people are always asked to be. The impossible strong. The strong where there's no space to think about your own vulnerability. The space to cry.

I look around the room, this small motel room, and I look at the two women I have traveled here with. In my role as a counselor at Cleveland, I played such a particular role for them. Haewon, a junior when Richie entered their high school as a ninth grader, embraced him as her little brother. I held them both close to me, mentored them both, trained them to be organizers for justice in our communities, organizers against the prison industrial complex, organizers for human rights.

And Taina, Taina, who fell in love with Richie months before he was arrested, committed to him, which made me commit to her. When they decided to marry after learning of his sentence, I was the one to marry them. I had become ordained in 2004, primarily because I was determined to marry Queer people despite what was then marriage inequity in California and the nation. As time moved forward and marriage equity took hold, my ordination and desire to marry people expanded to include all those who for different reasons were prevented from legally being families. Including prisoners and their wives. I officiated Taina and Richie's service, their exchange of vows inside of jail, and there has not been a weekend in all the years that they've been together when she has missed seeing him.

So even though I am not so much older than they are, whether Richie or Taina or Haewon or even Trayvon, I am old enough to feel responsible. I have become my big brother Paul. I feel the weight of being with two Black women who are younger than me in this prison town, and I wonder, if it came down to it, would I be able to protect them, protect us? Do I have any power to ensure that they will live long— that their Black lives will be full and healthy?

I cannot stop myself from crying. As much as I want to. I weep hard. We all do. And then I get angry. Once again my world is defined by cognitive dissonance: to be in this town where this little boy, literally this 18-year-old boy, who had hurt no one, would be locked up for ten years and this white-presenting man could kill us and go home.

And then my friend Alicia writes a Facebook post. Alicia, who I'd known for seven years at this point, who I'd met at a political gathering in Rhode Island where at the end of

the day our goal was to dance until we couldn't dance anymore. She and I danced with one another all night long and
began a friendship that holds us together to this very day.
But she writes these words in the wake of the acquittal:

> btw stop saying that we are not surprised. that's a
> damn shame in itself. I continue to be surprised at
> how little Black lives matter. And I will continue
> that. stop giving up on black life. black people, I will
> NEVER give up on us. NEVER.

And then I respond. I wrote back with a hashtag:

#BlackLivesMatter

Alicia and I brainstorm over the course of the next few
days. We know we want to develop something. We know we
want whatever we create to have global reach. Alicia reaches
out to her friend Opal Tometi, a dedicated organizer who is
running Black Alliance for Just Immigration, based in Brooklyn, New York. Opal is a master communicator and develops
all the initial digital components we need to even get people
to feel comfortable saying the words Black Lives Matter, for
even among those closest to us, there are many who feel the
words will be viewed as separatist, that they will isolate us.
Opal pulls together the architecture for our first website and
Twitter accounts, our Facebook and Tumblr. We are determined to take public this basic concept: That our lives mean
something. That Black Lives Matter.

After a few days I return to Facebook and I begin to post.

I write that we are going to begin organizing.

I write: *I hope it impacts more than we can ever imagine.*

12

RAID

Most middle-class whites have no idea what it feels like to be subjected to police who are routinely suspicious, rude, belligerent, and brutal.

DR. BENJAMIN SPOCK

We lived in a tiny oasis village nation island in the center of the city that was called St. Elmo's, a Technicolor vision of love come to life under the Black and gentle hands of a man, an artist named Rozzell, and his nephew Roderick. In 1969 they saw an abandoned street and cracked concrete and convinced their local councilman, a Black man named Tom Bradley who would later become mayor, to envision a world with them, to believe that there could be a place where life could be lived in peace and in courage, in the full embrace of light and of human possibility, and a world where mighty redwoods could replace weeds, where gardens could be planted, which they were, gardens that survive to this day, along with the redwood that marks the start of the Village as testimony that despite war and despite conflict and despite hate and despair, there could be another way forward, there could be another way to dream, another way to coexist and if we wanted to walk on rainbows we needed only paint the concrete and embrace our own imaginations, which is what happened, and we walked on them, the rainbows, and we told the story of ourselves in murals that called out to whoever passed by we were here, we were fucking here and we were dreaming and supporting and believing and everything beautiful really was possible because we were possible and we were a safe harbor and telling you this now, writing it all down, does not begin to edge toward explaining what was taken from me when the raids made it impossible for us—for me—to live in the one place I found I could live—and live all the way—simply because we, because I, believed and demanded that police stop killing Black people.

The police helicopters sound closer than usual, and I speculate that this summer afternoon in 2013 they are coming into our Village, St. Elmo's, a collective of cottages in midcity LA where artists and organizers of color have lived and taught art to the community since the 1960s.

I tell JT, my friend and an artist who is visiting my home with his six-year-old daughter, that on top of the Black Lives Matter work, Dignity and Power Now has been pushing and demanding that the local sheriff's department be held accountable, making us very unpopular with law enforcement. Dignity and Power Now is part, now, of the larger Black Lives Matter network.

We were raided a few months ago, I tell JT. It was the first time police had ever entered our Village.

Our Village, where we have our own ecology, green succulents and cacti, and a Chinaberry tree proud in the center. This is my home, the first place where I have felt wholly safe, the place where I have felt whole. Mark Anthony and I moved here after living in the Canyon.

We rent out two cottages in the Village. Two cottages we have used to heal Monte. Cottages where we have organized. Our cottages where we have grieved. Where we have made love and been love. But the Village as a whole has been a meeting ground for hope, and now the helicopters we've been hearing since early in the day sound overhead.

In June 2013 Trayvon Martin's killer has not yet been acquitted and Alicia, Opal and I have not yet come together to form Black Lives Matter or shape it into a national and then international network.

There is nothing actually called Black Lives Matter yet, but there have been protests across the nation. There have been sit-ins. There has been the fight just to get the killer arrested. There has not been silence. Not in Florida or Oakland. Not in Chicago or New York and not in LA, where I live and have fought for the right to simply live since I was 16 years old.

JT, his daughter Nia Imani and I feel like small prey beneath a hawk. We still ourselves in a corner of the cottage. The helicopters seem like the loudest things we've ever heard. We speculate: Are they even monitoring anyone or is this just another reminder to us that we are a people under

siege? Another story that does not get told when they tell the
story of California is the story of occupation, of what it means
for so many of us who are Black or Latinx to live unable to
escape the constant monitoring by police, the idea that your
very existence, the brown of your skin, is enough to get you
snatched up, enough to get you killed.

We've always known this but in 2012 and 2013 we were
able to use to social media to animate a national conversation. But make no mistake.

We knew it when Oscar Grant was killed in Oakland,
sitting still and compliant on the floor of the Fruitvale BART
station.

We knew it when Amadou Diallo was killed. Forty-one
bullets. Some through the bottom of his feet.

We knew it when Sean Bell was shot and killed getting
into a car after his own bachelor party in New York.

We knew it when we read about Clifford Glover, a boy
of ten living in Queens, New York, in April 1973. Little
Clifford was shot by police while simply walking with
his stepfather down a street in their South Jamaica, Queens,
neighborhood. The killer cop, Thomas Shea, who was
acquitted, simply offered as his defense that he didn't see
anything except the child's color.

Ida B. Wells knew it when she risked her life to expose
the killers of Black men, women and children by white lynch
mobs that were populated by, and often led by and protected
by, Southern law enforcement.

The Deacons of Defense knew it when they organized
themselves to protect people from the tyranny of white

vigilantes and police in 1964 in Jonesboro, Louisiana, and then founded their first chapter in Bogalusa, Louisiana, on February 21, 1965, the day Malcolm X was assassinated.

And the Black Panthers knew it when Huey Newton and Bobby Seale, with two guns slung over their arms, organized in the name of self-defense against the Oakland Police Department in October 1966.

We were and are their progeny, called to pick up a torch no generation wants to or can ignore.

Police, the literal progeny of slave catchers, meant harm to our community, and the race or class of any one officer, nor the good heart of an officer, could change that. No isolated acts of decency could wholly change an organization that became an institution that was created not to protect but to catch, control and kill us.

The record was clear.

In the city of Los Angeles, almost 50 percent of *all* homicides go unsolved and gang injunctions did absolutely nothing to stave off violence in the street. Protection wasn't the goal no matter what anyone said.

In the state of California a human being is killed by a police officer roughly every 72 hours.

Sixty-three percent of these people killed by police are Black or Latinx.

Black people, 6 percent of the California population, are targeted and killed at *five times* the rate of whites, and three times the rate of Latinxs, who have the largest number of people killed by police.

Who is protected? Who is served?

When I am asked to speak at universities, in communities, I share these statistics. I tell them that even as we are labeled criminal, we are actually the victims of crime. And I tell them there are no stats to track collateral deaths, the ones that unfold over months and years spent in mourning and grief: the depression that becomes addiction to alcohol that becomes cirrhosis; or else addiction to food that becomes diabetes that becomes a stroke. Slow deaths. Undocumented deaths. Deaths with a common root: the hatred that tells a person daily that their life and the life of those they love ain't worth shit, a truth made ever more real when the people who harm you are never held accountable.

Unlike homicides that occur at the hands of non-police, when cops kill, there is the presumption that the killer is in the right, that his or her decision was reasoned and necessary and done in the name of public good and safety, not as a result of poor training and surely not as part of the long history of police violence rooted in racial hate—despite the fact that cops were created in this nation specifically *and solely* to hunt Black people seeking freedom.

Some version of all this peppers the whispers JT and I share during our time in the corner of the cottage with the helicopters hovering and the six-year-old terrified and us not able to explain things to her but also not able to say nothing at all. Finally I offer, *We're being still right now,* and JT, trying to comfort, whispers in my ear, *Maybe they are not coming for you this time.* We pause and then he says what we both know: of course that would mean they're about to swoop down in another Black or Brown corner of the city, one of many areas designated as an urban jungle, a place behind enemy lines and ground zero in the war on drugs. Where we live, children are defined as super-predators even by liberal politicians, none of whom pause when the response to that designation is to allow local police to use militarized responses and maneuvers on mothers and fathers, daughters and sons.

Two years later, we will not be shocked at the use of tear gas, assault weapons and tanks when we protest the death of unarmed Michael Brown, shot dead on the streets of Ferguson, some of those bullets entering the top of his head. The federal government has provided these to local police departments for decades, since at least the modern declaration of the war on drugs, and LA, my city, was where the first-ever SWAT raid was ever undertaken. A generation ago, it was another group of young Black activists, the Black Panthers, who had come together around police violence, who were in law enforcement's crosshairs.

But on the day of the helicopters I am focused on only these two immediacies: keeping us alive and centering myself enough to begin the familiar and terrible process of preparing myself mentally to have to respond to the news of another unarmed child being killed—and with impunity.

Or if there is an arrest and if they survive, will they be treated as Monte was treated, beaten and starved, locked in solitary confinement? Will they be disappeared as Monte was disappeared, only to reappear months later, perhaps even with the charges dropped but the trauma intact? I wonder if any of our kids ever get the proverbial slap on the wrist. The "C'mon son. You can do better than this." The "Let's go talk to his parents. Maybe he needs therapy." Did anyone in law enforcement ever say about one of our kids, "Jail would destroy him, so let's find another way to help." Did we ever get a first chance, let alone a second? What did Trayvon Martin get? What did Clifford Glover? Rekia Boyd, sitting in a Chicago park with friends in 2012, talking and laughing, when an undercover cop accosted them and shot her 22 years of life and possibility into oblivion?

I am thinking about all of this, and I am especially thinking about Monte and how grateful I am he is not with us in the cottages that day, when the banging on my front door begins.

Wait here, I say to JT. I cannot let him be the one to answer. As protective as he is of me—JT will become one of the first Black Lives Matter organizers—I know his dark-skinned, six-foot-four, 200-plus-pound frame will present as an opportunity, an excuse for violence.

If unarmed Trayvon Martin, sixteen and skinny, carrying iced tea and candy, could be shot down in cold blood walking home to his own house while he was on the phone supporting a girl who had been bullied . . .

If unarmed Oscar Grant could be shot and killed, sitting compliantly on the floor of the BART station with his hands on his head . . .

If unarmed Ramarley Graham could be shot in his own bathroom in front of his grandmother and little brother because cops claimed he had weed on him . . .

If all this is true, I know JT doesn't stand a chance. I know if he answers the door, it may be the last thing he ever does.

As the banging continues, I hug JT's small, dark chocolate girl, an emerging artist—she loves to paint. Nia Imani and I have built a special connection. I tell her everything will be fine. I crack the front door of our cottage just enough to slip outside. Know Your Rights workshops have long drilled into me not to let police in if they don't have a warrant, which I do not believe they do. We have done nothing wrong. Not that that stops brutality, but I hold on to it anyway and run through a list of what we have done:

We have joined the rest of the country in protesting in order to get Trayvon Martin's killer charged.

We have gone to meetings and held one-on-ones with community members.

We have painted murals.

We have wept.

We have said publicly that we are a people in mourning.

We have demanded they stop killing us.

But we have harmed not one single person nor advocated for it. They have no right to be here!

Even still, I am shaking. I am terrified. Outside my door, there are at least a dozen police in full riot gear. I am a single woman, unarmed and five feet two. Every single one of the people standing before me, their faces disguised by helmets, their bodies shielded in Kevlar, has a weapon trained on me or on my home.

A Latinx officer is the one who engages me.

Someone tried to shoot up the station, he begins. We think they may be hiding in one of the Village cottages.

No one is here, I say.

Why are you shaking then? he pushes, aggressive but not nasty.

Because your shotguns are pointed at me. Because all these guns are pointed at my home, I say, and gesture with my eyes not with my arms, another lesson from Know Your Rights.

I reassert, There's no one here you're looking for.

I open the door and re-enter, and back inside JT grabs me and hugs me and together we try to breathe.

Minutes pass, who knows how many, but we hear the police again. They are speaking right outside our window and, it seems, as loudly as possible. I recognize the voice of the Latinx officer who had been the one to address me.

I think she's afraid because someone is inside. Like influencing her, he says. I inhale deeply.

They are inventing a reason to come in even though they don't have a warrant, I say to JT, who agrees.

The banging on my front door begins again, and this time we are told that we are to come out. We are told we have no choice.

JT and I look at one another and we look at his tiny six-year-old girl. I wonder, is this how it ends for her, for us? I don't say this, of course. What we do say to one another is that we need to get out of this alive. We say situations much less charged than this have resulted in death, in needless death.

We decide that JT and Nia Imani exiting first followed by me is the safest way to leave. We pray that they will not harm a father and daughter but we know that if at any moment JT is alone, they will kill him.

I call out, My friend is here with his six-year-old daughter. They're coming out first.

They walk out. I follow.

Immediately, the police surround the three of us, who are not armed and who are dressed like three people who were sitting in their house and planning out their day, which is what we had been doing when we first heard the helicopters.

Ten, maybe a dozen, cops force us at gunpoint—and by we, I mean also six-year-old Nia Imani—into the courtyard in front of our cottage while the others swarm past us and enter my home like angry hornets or a sudden airborne plague. They are in my home for hours.

Detectives join them at some point and begin taking pictures of everything outside and, from what we can tell, inside my home. We have not been given a search warrant and we cannot protest. We are being held at gunpoint the entire time and are mostly blocked from watching what they do inside my home, what they take, what they leave. They treat my home the way they treat the jail cells my brother was locked in, a place where the police—guards—can remove you for any reason or no reason at all, at any hour, and tear up your belongings, with or without cause, take shit or leave it. And there's nothing you can say as pieces of your life are scattered or destroyed by what can only be experienced as a violent human tornado.

After three hours or four, without another word to us, they finally leave.

After that, I move out.

The first time the police ever entered St. Elmo's Village was in February 2013. We were gearing up for the trial of Trayvon Martin's killer, still months away, and on that chilly LA night, I had spent some rare time just kicking it with friends at a comedy show, and now it was late, maybe 1:00 in the morning, and I was heading back to my cottage where Mark Anthony was supposed to be sleeping but instead was standing outside our home, barefoot, in pajamas and with his hands cuffed behind his back.

Mark Anthony, the beautiful child of one of the original members of Earth, Wind and Fire. Mark Anthony, whom I've loved since I was 16. Mark Anthony, my soulmate. Mark Anthony, who had challenged himself and the privileges he enjoyed, a long, lean, light-skinned wave of a boy all the white girls wanted but who always chose us. He always chose Black girls. He always chose me. And now all we had read about and studied, all we were building our muscles to fight, had come crashing in through our bedroom door and dragged this beautiful healer outside and handcuffed him in the cold night air.

This is who the police yank out of sleep. They were able to gain entry to our home because in St. Elmo's, before this, we never locked the doors. But on this night, the police entered through our back door. They said he fit the description of a guy who'd done some robberies in the area. They offered no further explanation.

On this particular raid, there are only a few cops at my place, nothing like what we would experience in the second raid. I'm not so afraid as I am angry. Later when I hear others dismissing our voices, our protest for equity, by saying All Lives Matter or Blue Lives Matter, I will wonder how many white Americans are dragged out of their beds in the middle of the night because they might fit a vague description offered up by God knows who. How many skinny, short, blond men were rounded up when Dylann Roof massacred people in prayer? How many brown-haired white men were snatched out of bed when Bundy was killing women for sport? How many gawky white teens were stopped and frisked after Columbine or any of the mass shootings that have occurred in this nation, the immeasurably wide margin of them by young, white men?

What the hell is going on? I demand.

Ma'am, one of them begins, It's been robberies in the area and he fits the description—

I don't wait for them to finish their story of trouble in the neighborhood.

What are you talking about? This is my husband. He lives here, I say, trying to put forward a calm I do not feel.

The police back down, and by now members of the community, awakened by the commotion, have come to stand with us. Mark Anthony's cuffs are finally removed, but the police do not leave my home for another two hours, taking down all kinds of information about him, running his license, hoping to find any reason to take him away, this man they yanked out of his own bed in the middle of the night in the house where he lives in a community where he is loved.

Close your eyes and come close.

Try to imagine this with me:

You are a graduate student whose work is in Chinese medicine.

Your dream is to be a healer.

And maybe while you are sleeping in your wife's bed, which is in a cottage that is part of a cooperative village where artists live and children come for free painting classes, maybe you are dreaming that you are saving a life, and in the midst of that dreaming, you are yanked out of bed by armed men dressed in riot gear, who possess no warrant, who have snuck into your bedroom through an unlocked back door. Their only reasoning is that you "fit the description."

And who exactly gave that description? What other proof did they have? How did they know you were even sleeping in that bed, since the cottage is not in your name but your wife's? How is this different from tactics used by the SS, the KGB, the Tonton Macoutes? And who is the real criminal, the real terrorist, and how will they be held accountable? To this day, the stench of these questions lingers, the stench of rotting meat unaddressed, unanswered.

13

A CALL, A RESPONSE

Freedom, by definition, is people realizing that they are their own leaders.

DIANE NASH

If we know nothing else, we know that in the wake of the acquittal of Trayvon Martin's killer, we have to change the conversation. We have to talk very specifically about the anti-Black racism that stalks us until it kills us.

We begin to plan. Alicia and I start going back and forth on Facebook, and separately, she is also having conversations with Opal. I say, during one of our discussions, We should build a political project.

Yes! Comes her reply. This is more than a hashtag.

This is about building power. This is about building a movement, we agree.

All over, everyone has already been talking about the life

of a Black child, a life that mattered. In 2012, the Dream Defenders embarked on their incredible 40-mile trek to the statehouse and occupied it, and the Miami Heat took their iconic photo with their hoodies on. A collective of New Yorkers including Thenjiwe McHarris and Daniel Maree launched the Million Hoodies Movement to push for dignity and justice for us; and in Chicago, Black Youth Project 100, a Queer Black Feminist organization of 18 to 35 year olds, dedicated itself to leadership development. And what we need now, in this early phase, is to press forward with a wholesale culture shift.

And it has to begin internally within our own progressive movement. There are people close to us who are worried that the very term, Black Lives Matter, is too radical to use, alienating, even as we all are standing in the blood of Black children and adults. We continue to push, to be undeterred.

In New York, in the wake of the acquittal, Opal helps organize a major march across the Brooklyn Bridge that culminates in a 1,000-person sit-in in Times Square, the crossroads of the world.

In Oakland, Alicia leads protesters through the downtown business area, where they are set upon by police. The media ignores the hundreds of people who are still in pain from the murder of Oscar Grant in 2009 and who are peacefully marching. Instead they focus on one or two who are not peaceful and they wholly ignore law enforcement, who attack everyone.

And in Los Angeles, working primarily with women, many of them students from Cal State, I begin planning what will become the largest march I've ever planned up until that point. I put a call out on Facebook for people to come to St. Elmo's Village to meet—I haven't yet been run out of it by the second raid—and Thandisizwe Chimurenga, one of our most beloved local journalists and radio hosts, helps get people to come. She brings Melina Abdullah, who teaches Black Studies at Cal State, and Melina brings her students, and together we form the core of what will become the organizing committee for our march, indeed for who we are in LA; it is the beginning of the build-out of our Black Lives Matter–Los Angeles DNA.

We have an initial list of demands:

- Federal charges need to be brought against Trayvon Martin's killer
- Marissa Alexander, imprisoned for attempting to defend herself against her husband, a known abuser, has to be pardoned
- There can be no more new jail or prison construction in LA
- We have to have community control over all law enforcement

We decide, for that first march, to go to Beverly Hills, to Rodeo Drive, where the wealthiest and mostly white people shop and socialize. All the other marches had been in Black communities, but Black communities know what the crisis is. We want to say before those who do not think about it what it means to live your whole life under surveillance, your life as the bull's-eye.

And as we plan the march, I reach out to all my contacts and others to theirs: the Strategy Center, unions, the Community Coalition. Years later a friend, a veteran organizer, will ask me about security for the march, how we ensured our protection. She will weep when she hears my answer: we didn't think about that.

That is how they will disrupt the narrative, the work, she says. That is what J. Edgar Hoover and the FBI planned when he created the Counterintelligence Program. That one generation would be dead, jailed or too traumatized to be able to pass on what is needed to make us safe.

But in the meetings we have in the Village, our focus is how to get across the message of building power and ensuring healing that we want to bring. In my home, we, mostly women, talk about what we deserve. We say we deserve another knowing, the knowing that comes when you assume your life will be long, will be vibrant, will be healthy. We deserve to imagine a world without prisons and punishment, a world where they are not needed, a world rooted in mutuality. We deserve to at least aim for that.

We agree that there is something that happens inside of a person, a people, a community when you think you will not live, that the people around you will not live. We talk about how you develop an attitude, one that dismisses hope, that discards dreams.

We deserve, we say, what so many others take for

granted: decent food, food beyond the 7-Elevens and Taco Bells that populated the neighborhood that brought me forth. We deserve healthy, organic and whole food that nourishes the body and the brain, that allows for both the full course of energy and the full rest of sleep at the end of a day well-lived and balanced with service, love and dreaming. We deserve to know life without the threat of heart attacks at 50, or strokes or diabetes and blindness because the food we have access to and can afford is a loaded gun.

And shelter. We deserve that too. Not the shelter that's lined with asbestos in the walls, or walls that are too thin to keep out the cold. Not the shelter with pipes that pour lead-based water onto our skin, down our throats in Flint, in North Dakota, in New York, in Mississippi. In places that never make the news. We deserve the kind of shelter our hard work demands, homes that are safe and non-toxic and well-lit and warm. And a shelter that is not a cage, whether that cage is a prison or its free-world equivalent. A shelter where our gifts are watered, where they have the space to grow, a greenhouse for all that we pull from our dreaming and are allowed to plant.

We deserve to be our own gardeners and deserve to have gardeners. Mentors and teachers who bring the sunlight, the rain, the whispered voices above the seedling that say, Grow, baby, grow.

We deserve love. Thick, full-bodied and healthy. Love.

And we take that message to the people in Beverly Hills, on Rodeo Drive, the idea that, in this place and in this time, when hate and the harshest version of living dominate, when even the worst assaults are blamed on the victims, when bullying has become ever present, limitless, we have come to say that we can be more than the worst of the hate. We say that this is what we mean when we say Black Lives Matter.

And with a bullhorn in my hand, wearing my black tank top and purple skirt, which is my uniform these days, and with the ever-present helicopters hovering over us, I say that they, those who come for brunch, have to confront the police presence today but that this is our everyday. I say that we were not born to bury our children, we were born to love and nurture them just like they were, and, because of this, finally we had to acknowledge that in fact this is what we had been forced to do and we had been forced to do it for too long, for centuries too long. We say that those children, now our dead, now our Ancestors, are calling to us, Trayvon is calling to us and asking that we remember so that we at last make the change that deserves to be made, that has to be made. I ask the people who are lunching, perhaps spending more on a single lunch than many of us spend to feed our families for an entire week, to remember the dead and to remember that once they were alive and that their lives mattered. They mattered then and they matter now.

And then I ask the people there on Rodeo Drive in Beverly Hills to please just stop for a moment, to hold space for Trayvon Martin, to hold space for his parents left in grief and an unspeakable pain. And when I do that it seems like the police are going to pounce; they move in closer and closer and I am scared. But I ask again for a moment of re- membrance for Trayvon, and as far as I can tell, every sin- gle person within reach of my voice, and all of them white as far as I can see, puts down their champagne glass and their silver fork and stops checking their phone or having their conversation and then every last one of them bows their head.

For months, the conversations continue, mostly, although not exclusively, with women. Many of us are Queer, some are Trans. We commit to guiding principles:

- Ending all violence against Black bodies
- Acknowledging, respecting and celebrating difference(s)
- Seeing ourselves as part of the Global Black family and remaining aware that there are different ways we are im- pacted or privileged as Black folk who exist in different parts of the world
- Honoring the leadership and engagement of our Trans and gender non-conforming comrades
- Being self-reflective about and dismantling cisgender priv- ilege and uplifting Black Trans folk, especially Black Transwomen, who continue to be disproportionately im- pacted by Trans-antagonistic violence
- Asserting the fact that Black Lives Matter, all Black lives, regardless of actual or perceived sexual identity, gender identity, gender expression, economic status, ability,

disability, religious beliefs or disbeliefs, immigration status or location

- Ensuring that the Black Lives Matter network is a Black women–affirming space free from sexism, misogyny, and male-centeredness
- Practicing empathy and engaging comrades with the intent to learn about and connect with their contexts
- Fostering a Trans- and Queer-affirming network. And when we gather, we do so with the intention of freeing ourselves from the tight grip of heteronormative thinking or, rather, the belief that all in the world are heterosexual unless s/he or they disclose otherwise.
- Fostering an intergenerational and communal network free from ageism. We believe that all people, regardless of age, show up with the capacity to lead and learn.
- Embodying and practicing justice, liberation and peace in our engagements with others.

In our separate locations, we continue to meet, to think through how to infuse art and culture in our work, youth organizing, meetings and other logistics. We begin a list of local demands and add to the evolving national demands, which begin, not surprisingly, with slashing police budgets and investing in what actually keeps communities safe: jobs, good schools, green spaces. In every demand and in the faces of the people I meet in the streets, in the work, I see my mother and my brothers, my father and my sister. I am clear, we are clear, that the only plan for us, for Black people

living in the United States—en masse, if not individually—
is all tied up to the architecture of punishment and contain-
ment. We are resolute in our call to dismantle it.

We are firm in our conviction that our lives matter by
virtue of our birth, and by virtue of the service we have offered to people, systems and structures that did not love,
respect or honor us. And while we are cultivating this idea
in our respective meetings and our respective teams, we,
Alicia, Opal and I, do not want to control it. We want it to
spread like wildfire.

But if our goal is to change the culture, to even get people
to believe in and speak the words Black Lives Matter, that
first year is one of fits and starts. We are able to talk about
the horrifics as they roll out with regularity. We hashtag
names again and again.

Renisha McBride, a 19-year-old girl, was in a car acci-
dent on November 2, 2013. Dazed and in pain, she knocked
on the door of Theodore Wafer of Dearborn, Michigan. He
answered her cry for help with the business end of a shot-
gun, killing this hurt and unarmed young woman without
a thought.

John Crawford, a 22-year-old father, picked up a toy gun
in the toy section of a Walmart in Beavercreek, Ohio, two
days before Michael Brown was killed. He was shot and
killed by an off-duty police officer who was not indicted.

There was the stunning public murder of Eric Garner
on July 17, 2014, in New York City, and there was his haunting callout: *I can't breathe, I can't breathe.*

These moments, in particular Mr. Garner's murder because it was videoed by bystanders and went viral, animate our pain and rage and resolve but we still are speaking of the killings in individual terms. Each its own horrific, not yet seen as part of a movement that says Black Lives Do Not Matter.

It is a year and four days after Trayvon's killer was acquitted and Black Lives Matter was born, and we are still hard at work trying to get people to see that as much as there is a progressive movement for justice, there are those working just as hard for the opposite outcome, an outcome where only the fewest of lives matter at all.

We know that if we can get the nation to see, say and understand that Black Lives Matter, then every life would stand a chance. Black people are the only humans in this nation ever legally designated, after all, as not human. Which is not to erase any group's harm or ongoing pain, in particular the genocide carried out against First Nation peoples. But it is to say that there is something quite basic that has to be addressed in the culture, in the hearts and minds of people who have benefited from, and were raised up on, the notion that Black people are not fully human.

And if few were willing to accept this before—the American Movement *Against* Black Lives—August 9, 2014, changed that.

In Ferguson, Missouri, on that date, an 18-year-old boy named Michael Brown was chased by a police officer, Darren Wilson. We don't know why. Later, reports would accuse Mike Brown of a scuffle at a convenience store, but whatever truth there may or may not have been to that story, what is true is that that scuffle was not known when Wilson, like Trayvon Martin's killer, gave chase. Wilson would claim that, upon confronting the teenager, who was headed to college in a matter of weeks, he felt that his life was in danger. But Mike Brown was unarmed and autopsy reports confirm that not only was he shot in the hand and chest—presumably enough to stop him if he was charging at Wilson, which witnesses dispute—but also he was shot in the top of his head. Twice.

Mike Brown's body was left in the hot Missouri sun for four and a half hours following his murder.

Mike Brown, who in so many ways reminds me of Monte. Size, color, age when the police came for him to kill him: these all read as my brother. These stories read as unique, as shocking to so many in this country, but to the people I know, these are the public assaults—when they are not outright executions—of our family, of the people who loved and nurtured us. I know it could always have been my brother left there on a street for hours, not only killed by a cop, but dishonored by a force of them.

Because what the autopsy did not reveal is that Darren Wilson's actions were part of a long chain of abuses visited upon the mostly Black, under-resourced and poor people who were and are the 21,000 residents of the city of Ferguson, a community in which the poverty rate is double that of nearby St. Louis. Law enforcement had, for decades, been able to do anything they wanted to do because who would speak up for a bunch of poor Black people? Who cared?

So horrifically were Black people treated that *The Atlantic* would run a 6,000-word report, following the Department of Justice's report on the ongoing abuses in Ferguson, in which journalist Conor Friedersdorf would write that,

> For years, Ferguson's police force has meted out brutality, violated civil rights, and helped Ferguson officials to leech off the black community as shamelessly as would mafia bosses.

Cops were pushed, required, not only to stop people—read: Black people—for the most minor incidents not related to public safety but also to issue as many citations as possible. It became a game—who could issue the most? Each citation carried a fine, and those fines made up the municipal budget. And there was no chance of fighting this economic warfare—because doing so could also lead to a person's arrest and jailing. The police chief sat over the municipal court.

In one case, a Black woman (almost all the cases involve Black people) ended up jailed over a first-time parking infraction. She was issued two citations that carried hundreds in fines and fees. She was poor and at times homeless, which caused her to miss court dates, which caused her to be arrested and spend time in jail. She tried to make partial payments, but without the ability to work out a payment plan, she was subject to arrest. Eventually the court relented and let her make payments, although seven years after the parking infraction, she is still in debt to the city of Ferguson for more than $500.

Friedersdorf reported another case that was cited in the DOJ report of a young Black man who lost his job after an arrest. In that case, the reporter shared that:

> In the summer of 2012, a 32-year-old African-American man sat in his car cooling off after playing basketball in a Ferguson public park. An officer pulled up behind the man's car . . . and demanded the man's Social Security number and identification. Without any cause, the officer accused the man of being a pedophile, referring to the presence of children in the park, and ordered the man out of his car for a pat-down, although the officer had no reason to believe the man was armed. The officer also asked to search the man's car.
>
> The man objected, citing his constitutional rights. In response, the officer arrested the man, reportedly at gunpoint, charging him with eight violations of Ferguson's municipal code. One charge, Making a False Declaration, was for initially providing the short form of his first name (e.g., "Mike" instead of "Michael"), and an address which, although legitimate, was different from the one on his driver's license. Another charge was for not wearing a seat belt, even though he was seated in a parked car.

At the moment Jim Crow's back was broken, American politicians found myriad other ways—all legislated, all considered legal—to ensure that the terrorism that had always been the primary experience of Black people living in the United States continued. And for a long time it continued with the broad silence of the people most harmed, which is to say, us. We did not rise up in numbers as we were written off as thugs, crack hos, welfare queens.

We used those terms ourselves! Our politicians and preachers used those terms! If slavery and Jim Crow made public spectacle of our torture—people beaten, whipped, lynched and dismembered for all to see—the last part of the twentieth century and start of the twenty-first century silenced us with false promises that if we just shut the fuck up and did what we were told, maybe we'd be Oprah or Puffy or LeBron, or, dare we say it, Barack Obama, when the truth was that the overwhelming majority of us spent a good portion of our time battling white supremacy, whether we knew it or not.

Because in Ferguson, like in cities across America, not only could the police extort Black people through the citation process for minor infractions, they also had at their disposal the huge unwieldy set of laws that made up what is known as asset forfeiture, a three-billion-dollar industry invented as part of the architecture of the drug war.

Asset forfeiture allowed law enforcement to seize property simply if they said that they suspected someone of being involved with the drug trade. They needed no proof or indictment even to seize cash, cars and homes, and police across the nation routinely did, leaving the burden of evidence on the person who was robbed. The victim had to prove that they had never done anything, something almost impossible to do. But even when they managed to fight and win their case, the legal barriers to reclaiming property were and are extraordinary, leaving the police, who were free to keep 80 percent of what they seized, to go on buying sprees. And what did they purchase most often? Military equipment. Another way of saying this is that the police in Ferguson stole from the residents and then used that money to buy the tanks, tear gas and machine guns that on August 9 would be turned against those very same residents.

And the images that first come out stun us; in particular, one.

There is a young Black girl and she is standing in front of a tank. A *tank!*

And in her hands she is holding a sign.

It reads simply this: Black Lives Matter.

We are a generation called to action.

14

#SAYHERNAME

We have chosen each other
and the edge of each other's battles
the war is the same
if we lose someday
women's blood will congeal
upon a dead planet
if we win
there is no telling

AUDRE LORDE

We know we have to go to Ferguson. We have to go in solidarity. Alicia and Opal and I are talking, along with Darnell Moore, the professor and master communicator, about how we can be in service. Darnell will help build out the Black Lives Matter network, but that will come later and Ferguson is burning now.

I reach out to organizers we know in St. Louis and the reaction about our coming is mixed. They are literally in the middle of a war zone. Some tell us come right away, but others are clear: only come if you are a lawyer, a youth organizer, versed in policy, can provide medical and other healing support or are a journalist. The activists on the ground, mothers and fathers, the family members, friends of Mike Brown, his community, are being called looters and thugs in the mainstream media. I call and text organizers from around the country and update them, and then, in conversation with Darnell, he suggests and we agree: let's pull together a Freedom Ride to Ferguson. We plan it for Labor Day weekend, two weeks away.

We set up a criteria-driven Facebook invite, and regional leads coordinate the vans and busses that will head from Northern and Southern California, Texas, New York and beyond to Ferguson. Monica Dennis in Brooklyn. Logan Cotton in Texas. There are so many people who go without payment or sleep to ensure our people in Ferguson get what they need in terms of support. We host a national call to lay out the idea and the logistics. Hundreds join.

We raise $50,000, primarily through CrowdRise, to offset the cost of busses and to pay for food for people once we arrive. We are in constant touch with the 15 to 20 people in Ferguson and the St. Louis area with whom we work most closely, but no one more so than one sister, Cheraaz Gorman, who has been on the ground since day one. She is our guiding light for the work in Ferguson.

A week before Labor Day weekend Darnell; Tamara,

Darnell's cousin who is a logistics magician; Tanya, my friend from high school; Coerce, a friend of Darnell's and an organizer originally from St. Louis but who has been living in LA; and I fly to St. Louis. We rent a car and drive to Ferguson, which is like driving into an occupied zone. Law enforcement from multiple municipalities is there. The National Guard is there. There are tanks on street corners. Even Los Angeles with its constant cop drive-bys and helicopters does not prepare me for this. My God, I think. All the money put in to suppress a community. We'd need far less to ensure it thrived. Where are the politicians who are doing that? I breathe deeply, intentionally, we all do, as we get in the car and head to meet with local organizers in advance of the Ride.

But in the car, a reprieve: We turn on the local popular radio station and in between playing Hip Hop, we hear them talking about Mike Brown. Talking about him with love. We're shocked. When we have heard our own local popular radio stations talk about us, it's always been with disdain. Could it be that we matter?

We're struck by, and discuss, the stark difference, too, between Ferguson and Sanford, Florida. Trayvon Martin was killed in a gated community, a place where people do not have the same familial relationships with one another, a place intended to separate people, section them off. Which is not to say that people were not outraged about Trayvon, but not until outsiders raised the issue first, elevated the pain his parents, his friends were meant to be left to deal with alone.

But here in Ferguson, Mike Brown was part of the

fabric of a community not sectioned off by gates. He was known here. Here, he was loved. We see people out in the streets, in small groups, in larger ones, sometimes by themselves. They are wearing Mike Brown t-shirts. They are hosting small protests or teach-ins. One person holds a Prosecute Darren Wilson sign. There is graffiti on walls that reads simply and boldly: We Love Mike Brown.

We drive by slowly, we nod at the organizers. We offer our respect.

Cheraaz is waiting for us at the local HBCU, Harris Stowe University, where she's set up a meeting with the president, who says we can use the school on Labor Day weekend as a central meeting ground for the Riders. We're thrilled and grateful and leave our meeting to identify hotels for people to stay in, and then we do meet-and-greets with local organizers along with members of the Dream Defenders and Black Youth Project 100 (BYP100). It's the first time I meet Umi Agnew and Charlene Carruthers, who started BYP100 to galvanize young organizers, 18 to 35, and build power using a Queer, feminist lens. I feel like I am meeting long-lost family. After two days, we feel like we have the lay of the land. We fly home to finish organizing the Riders.

And then two days before the Ride, the president of Harris Stowe is a ghost. I call and call and cannot reach him. Finally a colleague of his responds to me. I don't know what you're talking about or what happened in that meeting. But our campus is closed Labor Day weekend. You cannot come here, she says. She is not rude but she is definitive.

I call Cheraaz and tell her I will figure something out and while I sit there in a panic, my telephone rings.

Hello, a voice I do not know says, Is this Patrisse Cullors?

Yes, I say.

My name is Reverend Starsky D. Wilson. I'm the pastor at St. John's United Church of Christ in North St. Louis. I heard you are looking for a central place to host the Riders. You can use my church.

I pause. And then: Many of us are Queer, are Trans, are gender non-conforming.

Reverend Starsky does not pause. All of you are welcome at my church, he says.

With quickness, we switch it up: through text, through Facebook, on Twitter. We send out a press release and hold a final call with nearly 600 organizers from all over the United States. Thenjiwe and Maurice, who will go on to found Blackbird Communications with Merv, another organizer, have been working on the ground tirelessly with the main local group, Organization for Black Struggle. We tell people about the pastor in North St. Louis who is giving us a home. I tell them about his spirit, his shine, his love.

Busses and vans leave on the Thursday before Labor Day. Fourteen hours for folks coming from New York, 38 hours for Californians. A team arrives from Toronto. There's a van organized by Black Transwomen who live in Ohio. Aaryn Lang, Wripley Bennett and Cherno Biko. They risk their

lives driving through the heartland, away from their designated safety zones, to come to support the people of Ferguson, to pay respects, to help. Later, they will tell us we did
little to ensure their visibility, to lift up the fact that our work
is being advanced by an extraordinary number of Transwomen and men. The most criminalized people on the
planet are Black Transwomen who cannot pass. We resolve,
as a movement, to ensure that that never happens again.
After Ferguson, when we speak of ourselves, we always lead
with this, that not only are we unapologetically Black, a term
coined by BYP100, but we are also Queer- and Trans-led and
non-patriarchal. We work with Lourdes Ashley Hunter, who
is the national director for the Trans Women of Color Collective. We also work with Elle Hearnes, who is now the executive director of the Marsha P. Johnson Institute. Black Lives
Matter is pushed to follow the leadership of Black Transwomen. Sometimes we fail and sometimes we succeed. After
Ferguson, we affirm that we must always have an evolving
political framework, that Black people are evolving so our
work—and each of us—must be evolving, too.

But we, our dynamic group of 600 organizers, lawyers,
policy experts, youth organizers and healers, arrive at Reverend Starsky's on Friday night. For the first time, I lay my
eyes on Opal Tometi, whom I've only spoken to over the
phone; we embrace. But it's anticlimactic in a way. We are
clear that we are in a war zone and that there is work to do.

Darnell and I take the stage and welcome everyone. We
review our guidelines about how to be with one another,
how to protect and keep one another safe. And in the base-

ment of Pastor Starsky's church we break bread, then head
to our hotels and Airbnbs and prepare to head to Ferguson
the next morning. The protests in Ferguson are around
the clock and by 10:00 A.M. our people—including Black
journalists like Brittney Cooper, Akiba Solomon and Jami-
lah Lemieux—are out there with them, standing shoulder
to shoulder against the tanks, the machine guns. We have
already learned from people in Palestine to douse our
eyes with milk, not water, when attacked with tear gas.

On Saturday evening, there are breakout protests everywhere and some of our people go to them. They head, with
local organizers, to the police station and begin their own
occupation—although ours, unlike law enforcement's—is
an unarmed occupation. It is a call for justice: Darren Wilson has still not been arrested, let alone charged, with Mike
Brown's murder. It will be months before we find out that
in fact, he won't be.

For those who do not go to the police station, we determine to create a space of respite for the community, and
Cheraaz gets the word out. We reconvene at the church and
community members begin to show up early that evening.
The people of Ferguson have been on the street and under
military assault for four weeks at this point. They have been
demonized in the media. They—we all—need a space to
speak, to be heard, to breathe. Mostly women are the people
who come together that night. Among those gathered are
Johnetta Elzie, Ashley Yates, Brittney Ferrell and Alexis
Templeton. But Larry Fellows is there as well. All are primary
organizers of the protests.

In the church there is the collective sense of overwhelm, of all the deaths and injustices that have led up to that August 9. In that room in that church we talk about CeCe McDonald, a Bi Black Transwoman who was sent to prison for defending herself after a man slammed her in the face with a drink at a bar. Cece ran out to get away from the man; he chased her and she fought back, stabbing him with a pair of scissors she had in her bag. He died and she was sent to prison, convicted of manslaughter. Like Marissa Alexander, sent to prison for firing her gun into the air to warn off her abusive husband—whom she'd gotten a restraining order against. No one was harmed, but in the same state that let Trayvon Martin's killer go, Marissa was sent to prison. She had no right to stand her ground. We talk about Trayvon and some of us talk about our little brothers. Some women talk about their lovers and remember Oscar Grant. Some talk about their fathers and remember Eric Garner. And Monte, Monte, he is with me in that room. Is with me in that city.

And then one by one the women talk about their own experiences, which mirror ones that we all have known: poverty, abusive relationships, communities under siege. I am reminded why I will forever insist that in our work we must always make space to confront trauma and to consider strategies for resistance. At some point, sisters begin to talk about how unseen they have felt, how the media has focused on men but it has been them, the sisters, who were there. They were there in overwhelming numbers—just as they were during the Civil Rights Movement. Women, all women, Transwomen, are roughly 80 percent of the people who are standing down the face of terror in Ferguson, saying We are the caretakers of this community. It is women who are out there, often with their children, calling for an end to police violence, saying We have a right to raise our children without fear. But it's not women's courage that is showcased in the media. One sister says, when the police move in, we do not run. We stay. And for this, we deserve recognition.

Their words will live with us, will live in us as Ferguson begins to unfold and as national attention begins to really focus on what Alicia, Opal and I have started. The first time there is coverage of Black Lives Matter in a way that is positive is on Melissa Harris-Perry's show. She does not invite us. It isn't intentional, I'm certain of that, and about a year later, she does. But in this early moment, and despite the overwhelming knowledge of people on the ground who are talking about what Alicia, Opal and I have done—and despite it being part of the historical record that *it is always women who do the work, even as men get the praise*—it takes a long time for us to occur to most reporters in the mainstream. Living in patriarchy means that the default inclination is to center men and their voices, not women and their work.

That fact seems ever more exacerbated in our day and age, when presence on Twitter, when the number of followers one has, can supplant the everyday unheralded work of those who, by virtue of that work, may not have time to tweet constantly or sharpen and hone their personal brand so that it is an easily sellable commodity. Like the women who organized, strategized, marched, cooked, typed up and did the work to ensure the Civil Rights Movement, women whose names go unspoken, unknown. So too did this dynamic unfold as the nation began to realize that we were a movement.

Opal, Alicia and I never wanted or needed to be the center of anything. We were purposeful about decentralizing our role in the work. But neither did we want nor deserve to be erased. I could tell you it was painful to watch the story of Black Lives Matter told without us, but the truth is that it was enraging.

I talk about it, our erasure, with Black women journalists, including Akiba Solomon of *Colorlines* magazine, who tells our mutual friend—and my co-author—asha bandele. asha has worked with and for *Essence* magazine for almost 15 years.

Tell me the whole story, asha says to me one day in late 2014. Tell me what people are not hearing.

She takes down my thoughts, my memories, my history and turns them into a brief essay for my approval.

Two months later *Essence* features a cover that for the first time in its history has no image, only the words BLACK LIVES MATTER. In it are my words. This is the first time that Alicia, Opal and I have our story told in a national publication—and it should be no surprise that it is a magazine dedicated to lifting up Black women.

I tell people what happened, who gave us space, who thought our work mattered, over and over. I tell people over and over how we need a sacred circle in order to do our work. Beyond lovers and BFFs, we need people who just love and support us without asking for anything in return except that we keep going. Alicia and Opal have each been held by their own circles of love and support, and when I set about this journey, and to this very day, I have been held by three veteran organizers and writers: asha, dream hampton and Rosa Clemente. They provide advice, make connections and often just listen when I need to talk something through. And I name them here because just as I would not be erased on their watch, neither will they be erased on mine.

On Sunday morning Reverend Starsky holds service, and many of us join all the usual members of the congregation. The service is a special one, dedicated to Black Lives Matter and the Movement. The choir opens up with a song: "We Need You to Survive." And Reverend Starsky gives a sermon that was written in the heavens as much as it was written here. He calls us all to action, says we stand with and for one another, for our community. And at the end of the sermon, when congregants are typically asked to come forward and commit to Jesus in their lives, Reverend Starsky gives us our mandate. He asks everyone, the entirety of his church, to come forward and commit to the Movement.

After that we fan out into the streets, some people back to protests, some to the neighborhood of the prosecutor, Bob McCullough, where we pass out flyers and talk to his community. *Tell him to indict Darren Wilson, the killer cop.*

On our final day in Ferguson, and in response to the community, we host a discussion on patriarchy in the Movement. Darnell pulls it together. He knows that even as a Gay, feminist Black man, he will be granted more space than he has earned, he says. We speak with organizers from the area who have gathered there and talk about what it means to step back, what it means to be an ally.

Meanwhile, Mark Anthony, Prentis Hemphill and Adaku Utah have converted the basement of the church to a healing justice space, and people who have been protesting for weeks walk into a room lit low with candles where a crew of healers is at the ready to provide massage, acupuncture and talk therapy. There is an art station where people can paint and draw what they cannot name or speak. There is an altar for people who have passed. There are pillows for people to rest on. We refuse to allow anyone or anything to make us less than wholly human. And in the fullness of our humanity, we need this, too, along with protests, and the deep discussions and policy pushes and theory, a place to rest, to renew. A place to restore.

And before we take our leave, we offer one more piece, a chant I shout at the top of my lungs from another woman this nation meant to erase but who would not be erased, Assata Shakur. In the center of the room, I shout for the first time publicly these words as loudly as I can, with people echoing them after each line:

IT IS OUR DUTY TO FIGHT FOR OUR FREEDOM!

IT IS OUR DUTY TO WIN!

WE MUST LOVE EACH OTHER AND SUPPORT EACH OTHER!

WE HAVE NOTHING TO LOSE BUT OUR CHAINS!

The work grows exponentially. In the December following Mike Brown's murder, Alicia, Opal and I meet together in

South Central LA, to begin talking about building out a network. People want to form their own chapters of BLM, take the work on locally. On our last day in St. Louis, we'd broken out into regional groups to see what people wanted to do and could do. But we also had people gather by areas of expertise: lawyers, journalists and healers met to coordinate how they wanted to serve. People hosted events in their cities to talk about Ferguson, what really happened. Coverage of who we were shifted to our messaging, not the imposed messaging filtered through mainstream media. We come together that first year on calls at least twice a month—hundreds of people—to talk about next steps, the most immediate of which is getting Darren Wilson indicted.

Yet as the work grows and people lose any hesitancy in saying that our lives matter and there are even folks in other countries looking to be part of what is becoming known broadly as the Black Lives Matter Movement, maintaining my closest relationship proves more of a challenge.

All my life, as a witness to my mother's life, I'd known love to be expressed as labor. My mother was not a cuddler, not a woman who demonstrated lots of emotion. After she and Alton broke up and until I was well into high school, I did not see my mother with a man, did not see her date. I suppose I thought she was asexual.

And while I am far more emotional than she, far more, in this regard, like my father Gabriel's family, like my mother who worked around the clock to do everything she could to ensure her family, I do, too. This is to say that Mark Anthony and I, despite our true and genuine love and respect for one another, begin to feel far more like friends than lovers, than husband and wife.

For six months I ask him to go to couples' counseling with me and for six months he says he will, but he never does. The romance and physical intimacy, once so much a part of our lives, fades, becomes a song associated with another time and place. I'm sure it doesn't help that we are also living with the anxiety that takes hold when a person is waiting for the next crisis to unfold. The whole world began to feel like a city under siege and when I think about it now, I think about how what we learned in that time was how to work together, but not how to love together. It is hard to be intimate with one person when you're being intimate with the world.

We never fight, Mark Anthony and I; fighting is not our way with one another and I wonder later if maybe it would have helped. Did I feel that while Mark Anthony would always fight alongside me, it was also true that he wouldn't fight *for* me, wouldn't fight to keep me in his life as a wife and lover? I think I did. I suspected—perhaps I had always suspected—that I loved him and wanted him more than he did me.

I take him to dinner one night at a favorite restaurant of ours, a Korean barbeque place near our home.

We're not working, I say.

I know, he says.

I love you, Mark Anthony, I say.

I love you, too, he says.

But we have to do our relationship another way, we agree.

After that, mostly silence. Silence and so much sadness. I am so very sad. We are transitioning, and while it is needed, it is painful. But we refuse to dis-acknowledge the role we'd played in each other's histories and development. We refuse to pretend we are not still connected, as family. We know it just has to be family in a new way.

No longer living as husband and wife, no longer lovers, Mark Anthony and I continue to work together closely, particularly around Dignity and Power Now. I spend most of my time raising money as he builds the health and healing programs in the organization. Here, in this way, we soar. We still do.

I begin to date again. I want to love, I need to love. I want a family, a core, a loving and stable center to return to, to awaken to. Carla introduces me to Rei, a Transman who is part Paraguayan, part Japanese. They are a brilliant urban planner and organizer, but I do not want to be monogamous and that isn't something they can deal with. At the time, I am also seeing JT, long a friend. He is the second and the only other cisgender, heterosexual man I have ever been with. He has been an integral part of the growth of BLM in its earliest stages and we are close. I care for him deeply as I care for his daughter deeply, the small artist who was with us during the second raid on St. Elmo's Village. JT and I begin to talk about what it would mean to have a child together. He wants another baby and I want to be a mother. We think about ways we could co-parent and partner without being married. I like

how I feel in the space with JT, both liberated and connected.

But while we are thinking aloud about children and
family, there is another July 13. It is 2015. We begin to hear
about a young woman who was driving to a new job and a
new life in Texas, where she would be an administrator at
a college. She had a vlog and she called it Sandy Speaks. She
offered opinions and comments on the state of our lives in
America. She challenged us: Are you doing something productive today?

She is one of us and her name is Sandra Bland and we
come to know her because on July 10, 2015, she was pulled
over for a nonsense traffic violation by a state trooper, Brian
Encinia. He claims the 28-year-old woman from Chicago
failed to signal a turn, and then, even as she is giving him the
documents he needs to write her ticket, he tells her to put
out the cigarette she is smoking *while sitting in her own car*.
She refuses, at which point Encinia snatches her out of the
vehicle and slams her to the ground on the side of the road.
The dashcam video of him doing this will circulate, along
with his subsequent rough arrest of her; Encinia threatens to
"light her up."

Eventually he will be indicted for perjury and fired, but
this will not happen in time enough to save Sandra Bland.
On July 13, 2015, she is found dead, hanged, in her jail cell.
Her death will be ruled a suicide, but no one with sense will
believe this. Had she ever expressed pain, frustration, sadness? Yes. Is this the case with most Black people living in a
nation that openly hates us? Yes. But is there anything in her

profile to say she would kill herself in jail? No. Not. One. Thing. She was on the way to a new job. She was actively advocating for herself and other Black people. She was in fight mode. She spoke to her sister and they were pulling together bail money.

Sandra Bland did not, did not, did not commit suicide.

Sandra Bland believed that her Black life, that all of our Black lives, mattered.

She stood for us and she was us.

We refuse to be silent.

Immediately, the African American Policy Forum, led by the great civil rights attorney Kimberlé Crenshaw, began using #SayHerName to acknowledge the numbers of Black women who were victims of state violence. Indeed, the day after Sandra Bland was found hanged in jail, in Alabama, 18-year-old Kindra Chapman was found hanging in her cell. She'd been in there for 90 minutes, held on the charge that she'd stolen a cell phone.

But there were more, so many:

Tanisha Anderson, a 37-year-old woman struggling with mental health issues, died after Cleveland police slammed her head into the pavement outside of her family's home.

Miriam Carey, a 34-year-old dental hygienist who made a wrong turn near the White House and was fatally shot by federal law enforcement officers in 2013. While her baby was in the car.

Shelly Hilliard, a 19-year-old Black Transwoman from Detroit who is threatened with being thrown in a men's jail for smoking marijuana unless she turns over her dealer. She does, but the cops reveal to the sellers who informed on them and Shelly is killed, cut into pieces and the pieces of her precious body, set afire.

Rekia Boyd, a 22-year-old woman living in Chicago, was hanging out with her friends in the park when she was shot and killed by an off-duty police officer who said he'd received a noise complaint.

Shelly Frey, a 27-year-old mother of two, shot by Walmart security who accused her of shoplifting.

Aiyana Stanley-Jones, a child of seven, killed when Detroit police officers barged into her family's home with their guns drawn. They shot her in the head.

Kathryn Johnston, a 92-year-old woman, shot and killed by Atlanta cops who were on a drug raid. They came in shooting and only later realized they got the address wrong.

These few names are only part of a long, terrible list, but, like the horrific history of lynching in this country, when the story is told, women are often left out of it even as we are lynched, too. And some of the women are pregnant at the time of the lynching. Some have their unborn babies cut out of their wombs.

And with Sandra Bland, maybe because she looked like a sister we would see at one of our meetings, one of our marches.

And maybe because our movement is being led by women, Queer and straight, cisgender and Trans.

And maybe because she worked so hard to put her voice out there, pushing anyone to hear her say our lives matter.

And maybe because so many of us have family who have been harmed in jails and prisons but that harm has not become part of the broader public discussion about the *bind, torture, kill* that is part and parcel of the American system of incarceration.

And maybe because we just can't stand one more loss, and for days after hearing what happened to Sandy I personally battled to pull myself out of grief—she was one of *our* family—we know, I know, we have to Say Her Name.

We had to raise our voices for her as she raised her voice for us. The world was going to know what happened to Sandra Bland, our sister, our family.

Several of us begin talking. I speak to friends from the Dream Defenders, from our LA chapter of BLM—we've grown to be 20 chapters at this point. And I speak to friends who are a part of Mi Gente. They have an incredible group of people working in Phoenix, the epicenter of anti-immigrant hatred and bigotry. We decide to meet up at the Netroots conference—which is being held in Phoenix. And we are fairly certain that no one there is going to talk about the 28-year-old woman who was found hanged in a jail cell in Waller, Texas. So we decide to.

We don't do things then the way I would do them now. I don't tell the larger BLM network what is happening, or even Alicia and Opal. I am still getting used to what it means to be in a national spotlight. We aren't sure how we are going to get the message out, but less than a week after we find out about Sandra Bland's death, on a Sunday night, we meet up at the single soul-food place in Phoenix, a Black-owned restaurant called Lolo's Chicken and Waffles.

They know who we are and give us private space in the back to meet. And in between the hours of planning and strategizing about what to do, we sing gospel songs and we mourn. We laugh and we cry. By the end of the night Angela Peoples from the LGBTQ human rights organization GetEQUAL says, Y'all. They're gonna do a candidates forum. Bernie Sanders and Martin O'Malley are going to be there. We need to interrupt that.

And I say, We need to shut it down. And that was that.

The next day, I text Jose Antonio Vargas, the brave journalist who had been part of the *Washington Post* team that garnered a Pulitzer for its breaking coverage of the mass shooting at Virginia Tech, and who outed himself as undocumented, having been sent to the United States from the Philippines as a child to live with his grandparents. Jose is going to be moderating the candidates' forum shortly and because I know him, I have to tell him we are coming.

Okay, he says.

And with that, 100 of us from the Black Lives Matter Movement and the immigrant rights movement break up into two lines and enter the room where the candidates are speaking. Amber Phillips, an organizer and a woman with one of the most amazing voices anyone could ever hear, sets it off. She begins singing:

Which side are you on my people, which side are you on?
(We're on the freedom side!)

Tia Oso, a Nigerian sister from Arizona who worked with Opal's organization, Black Alliance for Just Immigration, hits the stage first. We wanted to begin by confronting the anti-immigration, anti-human positions Arizona has taken. Tia talks about Black immigrants in Arizona and the audience begins to boo. The audience of Democrats begins to boo. I am beside myself with anger. How dare they boo her for telling the truth! My mind begins to race, trying to figure out what to do next. I am standing there barefoot because I am part of the next phase of the action. I am not supposed to be onstage but I cannot let them treat Tia like this. I run up on the stage to stand with her and yell back at the audience: How dare you boo her, boo us?! Our people are dying! We are being killed! We. Are. In. A. State. Of. Emergency!

The audience stops booing. They start to listen. And our action continues.

One by one each of us finds a chair—this is why I am barefoot, why we came in barefoot. And one by one almost all of us begin to speak:

If I die in police custody, know that they killed me.

If I die in police custody, show up at the jail, make noise, protest, tell my mother.

If I die in police custody, tell the entire world: I wanted to live.

The video of our disruption makes international headlines. It is the first time I think I really understand the impact we are having. I leave Phoenix thinking about that and preparing for the Movement for Black Lives gathering that is being pulled together by a wide range of Black people and organizations that are determined to end state violence.

The MBL gathering is only a week away and it will be the first time that all of us will be in one space together. We've chosen Cleveland, Ohio, to come to because it has become Holy Ground, the place where little Tamir Rice has been killed. I want to spend the next week thinking about that, thinking about our own power and what our responsibility is. But before I can settle deeply into those considerations, there comes another one, and it is ever more immediate. Noticing I am a little late, I think, what the hell?

I take a test.

I am six weeks pregnant.

15

BLACK FUTURES

I didn't fall in love. I rose in it.

TONI MORRISON

I am home, back in LA after the Ohio gathering— and I am sick as shit.

I tell JT that I am going to take a pregnancy test. He is impassive. I don't understand but I go into the bathroom and within seconds the tell-tale plus sign appears. I rush out of the bathroom and then over to JT. I'm pregnant! I say.

His back is to me, facing his laptop. He does not turn around. He does not acknowledge I have spoken.

Did you hear me? I say. I'm pregnant!

I heard you, he says. He turns to me and the look I see on his face is fear, but also a deep well of sadness I cannot understand. I walk away, stunned, confused, disturbed.

I don't know how to respond to him, what to ask for,

what to say. We'd talked about wanting to co-parent, even as we knew we would not be monogomous. But we had talked about trying to build a family in the midst of the madness. Why is he behaving this way? Years of friendship—we had endured the second raid at St. Elmo's Village together!—and our recently emerging romantic relationship. I leave our home and go outside and call Future, who is one of the leads of BLM Toronto.

Future and I met in 2014 after Ferguson, through Google hangout. We were both all about the work, all about justice for our people. And in 2014, Toronto wanted to start a BLM chapter given Canada's own terrible history of Black people being killed by police. Most of the victims did not have guns, many were mentally ill and at least one was un-armed *and* suicidal at the point police shot him.

Future is Genderqueer and I immediately took to them. The first time we talked on Google hangout, our passion was mirrored, our determination to create another world for our people was the same. Between that first conversation and the many we would have until we meet face-to-face in June 2015, a month and a half before I learn that I am pregnant, our rela-tionship, care and respect for one another have been solid. And then we saw each other.

I'd gone to Canada for the Allied Media Conference and to perform as part of the Pride Festival. When I laid eyes on them, I was blown away by how gorgeous they were. Google hangout did not convey their beauty fully. But I breathed through it, breathed through our chemistry, which was electric. JT was at home after all and we were talking about having a baby.

I discussed my relationship with JT with Future, said that we were talking about having a baby. They couldn't have been more respectful. We continued to build our relationship, the personal one, the professional one. I asked them to help me celebrate my thirty-first birthday, which fell on June 20, while I was still in Toronto, and they agreed and together we created a quiet, private space on my thirty-first turn around the sun. We talked about our families. I told Future about Gabriel. I told them about Monte. I told them how much I wanted a child of my own.

Future told me about their childhood. They have a sister who is their twin and a brother. And they, all three, were split up by foster care; their mother had struggled with mental illness.

It wasn't easy, they said. And then they said, If having a baby is what you want, I will support you.

We are Queer and cannot take having a baby for granted in the way heterosexual couples can. And soon, I will learn how true Future is to their word when JT disconnects from me, from the baby. Future is the one who is present. Perhaps the call to Future on that day is some kind of unconscious test on my part. Does anyone mean what they say? In any case, they pass. With extra credit.

In fact, when JT rejects me, calling Future to tell them I am pregnant feels natural, feels right. Feels safe.

We've known each other for such a brief period of time

and I don't know what that thing is that connects one person to another. But whatever it is, we have it.

I'm pregnant, I say to Future that morning when JT
keeps his back to me. I do not tell them this about JT though.
I am embarrassed by his behavior. Embarrassed about what
it might say about me.

Future says simply, quietly, clearly, I am *so* happy for
you. What do you need? How can I support you? they ask.

And I exhale. Tears form in my eyes. We're going to be
okay, I think, and try to telegraph this to the tiny person
taking shape inside of me.

Days later, I have my first doctor's visit. JT says he will
come with me. But when it's time to get ready, he will not
come out of the bathroom. I won't beg. This is crazy and
not what we agreed on. I call Carla. In no time she is picking me up, taking me to the doctor. Everything is fine: the
heartbeat, the growth. I'm doing this. I'm having a baby.
I'm having *this* baby. This baby whom I am already in love
with. Not long after, I have a conversation with Future—
we are speaking daily at this point, but this discussion is especially significant.

Will you be present at the birth? I ask.

Of course, they say.

I tell them that I am scared about being alone and pregnant and in the middle of a movement that is fighting for
the lives of Black children.

Future talks about family, about what it means to have
that taken, as theirs was taken from them during the time
in foster care.

We agree that this is not the way either of us imagined we would start a journey of parenting.

We also agree that we love one another and this magical life incredibly growing inside of me. We—*we*—love that baby so deeply. Already.

Months later, after the baby is born, JT and I will commit to a beautiful, restorative mediation process and I will learn about the grief he had been hosting privately, grief he didn't know how to discuss or understand. His grandmother, to whom he was so close, was near death, and his most treasured uncle, who was also his father's twin, passed away. There was so much happening, he will say to me. There was all this public grief and I couldn't find space to understand my own personal sadness, my individual loss.

Post-partum and for the baby, we will promise to work for peace, but in the moment of pregnancy, we struggle, and almost immediately, JT and I stop living together. I spend the first trimester of my pregnancy couch surfing. Mostly Carla, always Carla, holds me down. As often as I can, I am in Toronto with Future, who is caring for me in a whole way. They are making sure I am eating. Helping me through my ever-present nausea and exhaustion. We are rising in love.

For the first time in a relationship, I feel completely taken care of. Emotionally, physically. Spiritually. I've had pieces of this in all my relationships but never the whole package, never the whole thing. Until Future. We find a two-bedroom apartment in West Hollywood that we love, an apartment with windows that have views. This will be

our home, we determine, but we have to first transition
Future from Toronto.

When I am five months pregnant we are ready to fully
make the move but we spend time, first, on vacation in Toronto. During our stay there, Future tells me that one of
their best friends is getting an award. They buy me clothes
to attend the ceremony, a fitted black dress, and even five
months pregnant, I feel gorgeous and sexy in it. We get into
Future's car and drive to their friend's house to pick them
up. Weird, I think. Why don't they have their own trans-
portation, I wonder, though fleetingly.

And then we walk in the house. Everyone yells, Surprise!!!!

Future had brought 15 to 20 of their closest friends
together and I think, Wow. They have community like I have
community. For months our relationship has been so one-on-
one, so internal, but here they are with all of their people. I
think we are having a going-away party for Future, who is on
their way to living with me in LA. But then all of a sudden
Future thanks everyone for coming, for supporting them, for
supporting us, and then they drop to one knee in front of me
and say, Patrisse, you are the love of my life. I knew it from
the day we met. Will you marry me?

And between laughter and tears, I say, Yes. Yes. And
Future slips a ring onto my finger, a simple rose gold band.

And just like that, we are engaged.

Days later while we are still in Toronto, I wake one
morning in excruciating pain. I can barely move, let alone
stand. A stabbing feeling radiates from my pelvic area and

completely debilitates me. Future rushes me to a clinic, where I receive the best health care I've ever gotten. When you go to the ER in the United States, the first place you are sent to is billing. In Canada I am sent, upon arrival, to a midwife, who examines me and does an ultrasound and assures me that the baby is okay. My fees are waived under the immigrant waiver fee—or something like that. I can hardly believe it. We learn, though, that what I do have is something called pelvic flooring disorder and that most of the pain will be alleviated with a belly belt. Future and I decide to fly back to LA and our apartment earlier than we'd planned.

At the airport we are sent to two different lines because our passports are different, our citizenship is different. I am wheeled through security, where I wait and wait for Future, who doesn't show up, and I am panicking. Finally, after several calls, I get through to them.

They won't let me in the country, Future says. I've been held back and questioned. That's why I couldn't call you.

It's hard to explain what some kinds of defeat feel like, how encompassing, how cruel, how hard to come back from. I am sitting in a wheelchair, unable to walk, six months pregnant now, and the person I love and rely upon most, the person I am engaged to, is being kept from me. Future is my consistency during my pregnancy, a pregnancy in which so little has been consistent. Not money. Not a home.

I want to break down but that is also not an option. I turn to the person who works for the airport who is helping me. Wheel me back, I say. Please, I say. And they do.

We are not going home. At least not yet. We get in a

cab and go back to Future's friend's house because that's where they'd been staying as we were making the full transition to the United States. Days later, I head back to my country of borders and walls. A country without my Future.

Carla picks me up from the airport and takes me to the apartment Future and I rented, which now feels immeasurably empty. She buys the belly brace to help alleviate the agony the pelvic flooring has left me in. Immediately, 80 percent of my pain is gone and it feels like I blink three times and my team has surrounded me to secure me during the weeks I will have to spend without Future. My friends Aura and Mesa show up, of course Carla and Tanya, my friend Noni comes through and so do dream and my mom. They cook for me and care for me and hold me down not only physically but also as we work with immigration lawyers to pull together the exorbitant amount of paperwork needed to bring my Future home to me.

Three weeks later, Future is on a plane, and after hours of harassment at the border, harassment that goes on for so long that they miss their flight and we have to buy a whole new ticket, we are together.

In February 2016, in the presence of our ancestors and 20 of our family and friends, in Malibu, California, at an Airbnb we had rented out and in my ninth month of pregnancy, Future and I are married.

We'd planned on marrying, of course, but the horrors with immigration at the airport sped up our decision. dream hampton officiates the wedding for us, and Future's brother and also their sister, their twin, are there. Carla and Merv and Tanya and Noni bear witness to our vows, as do Future's closest friends from Toronto: Allix and Anu, and Future's best friend, Matt. Among those gathered in the crowd is Mark Anthony, my family forever, my cherished friend. He takes me in his arms.

I am so happy for you, he says, and in the background the waves of the mighty Pacific waters crash against a new shoreline.

Three and a half weeks later, at midnight on March 21, I go into labor a day early. I call my midwives and family and I stay at home and labor for 15 hours, 16. And then I stop dilating.

I know my baby is breech and I have a doctor on call who does breech home births. But then the contracting stops. Don't worry about it, my doctor and my midwife say. Just go to sleep. Let's see what happens.

The next morning when I awaken I am still not contracting. My mother and Future are there with me and as much as I want my baby to be born at home, I also know we have no choice. We rush to the hospital and on March 22 at 1:00 in the afternoon, my Shine is born. Future is there throughout the C-section, there at the birth: one precious thing we'd fought for has at least come to pass. I am in a world of pain after the birth—the doctors refuse to give me as much pain medication as I need—but I cannot stop staring at Shine, our own Black Future.

We are in the hospital together for four nights and five days, and finally I am told we can go home. Mom comes home with me and stays with us for the first two nights and we marvel: This baby is so gentle, so sweet, rarely crying. I want to hold him forever in my arms, keep him safe from the world, run away to a place where only love lives. I am a mother now, and like any mother, as vulnerable as I've ever been but as strong as I've ever been, as well. We, Future and I, make a family decision two weeks after Shine is born. In Toronto, BLM has occupied the police station. They are calling for charges to be brought against the cops who killed Andrew Loku, an immigrant from the Sudan, a father of five, a man without a gun. Future helped create our team in Toronto, helped lead them. I feel like I have to be there, they say to me.

I do, too, I say, Shine in my arms.

And after that, Future leaves for three weeks, heads into one battlefield as I remain in LA with our baby, at the ready, on still another one.

16

WHEN THEY CALL YOU A TERRORIST

If you hear the dogs, keep going.
If you see the torches in the woods, keep going.
If there's shouting after you, keep going.
Don't ever stop. Keep going.
If you want a taste of freedom, keep going.

HARRIET TUBMAN

On November 8, 2016, we are in downtown LA at an election-night gathering. It's being hosted by Lynne Lyman and asha, who have brought me into the campaign to legalize marijuana in the state. They are determined to include the voices and opinions of the communities most impacted by the drug war. It's not just the destination, Lynne says to me, it's also the journey, and this has to be a victory owned by community.

Marijuana is the first point of contact so many young

people have with police, contact that often sends them spiraling deeper into the claws of the prison industrial complex. In California, marijuana is the fourth leading cause of
deportation, and every night in LA County 500 people sit
in the jail simply for possessing it. It's ridiculous and the le-
galization law I have worked to support will mean that no
child will ever go to prison for marijuana again, that people
with a marijuana conviction will not be automatically kept
from participating in the marketplace, and that 50 million
dollars a year from tax revenue generated by its legal sale
will be invested in communities harmed by the drug war.
And after months of pushing and canvassing and working
to get the word and the vote out, months when our poll
numbers dipped down, but then started trending up in the
final two weeks, by 8:00 P.M. on election day, it's clear that
we're going to win and take one more tool out of the arse-
nal that is used to incarcerate and criminalize mostly young
Black and Brown people.

But it also looks like Donald Trump is going to win the
presidency, and as the night wears on, we realize this is exactly what is about to happen. A man who openly cam-
paigned on bigotry, white supremacy and misogyny is about
to be elevated to one of the most powerful positions in the
world. I slide down a wall in the corner of the room. asha
brings us drinks and takes a long swig of water. She and
Lynne have to hold it and us together; they still have to an-
nounce our victory and, at the stroke of midnight, celebrate
the first person, Ingrid Archie, to file to have her record for
a marijuana conviction expunged, because the law makes

that possible, too. We tried to think of everything, tried to undo as much injustice as we could in this single piece of legislation, Proposition 64. And we have done it but it feels like everything else has gone straight to hell. How will we survive a Trump presidency? How will we ever protect the people we need to protect? And what about my own child? My own little Shine? Despondent, Future and I leave the gathering and head home to consider the tomorrow we personally, along with our community, will face while Opal holds space with the undocumented families she fights for daily and Alicia remains steadfast, unbowed and ready for battle. She is in full-on planning mode.

It takes me longer to get there. There are moments in each of the days and weeks that follow the election where I cannot stop the tears from pushing, the fear from rising up like bile in my throat. But I am not crying for myself. I am crying for our families still living in poverty. I am terrified for Monte and all the people like him whose health care is at risk. I am crying because for the first time in my life as an organizer, I actually feel helpless. On November 9, there was nothing I could do to stop this man from being president.

And then I get angry. Because we've tried so hard. Ninety-six percent of Black women tried so hard in voting against him. And not only did this country not elect Clinton, it elected a person who publicly supported sexual assault, a man once accused of rape by his daughter Ivanka's mother. I am angry with the Democratic Party for not knowing that there could have been and should have been a better candidate and angry that a better campaign—a campaign that honored the journey, that included community in real and transformative ways—was not launched. I am angry I didn't realize—or accept at a cellular level—how wedded to racism and misogyny average Americans are. I am angry at my own naiveté. Our own naiveté. There was a real and substantive difference between these two candidates and we didn't take that seriously enough. Hell, I hadn't believed Trump would even beat the Bush legacy candidate, and then that candidate was one of the first he knocked out.

But in the wake of the election, it is important that I look in the mirror, that we all do. His campaign and election has put all of our lives even more at risk. In 2016, hate crimes in the United States rose 6 percent in 25 of the largest cities. And we, Black people, were the most common target of them, with hate crimes directed at us disproportionately, at nearly 30 percent, according to FBI statistics.

Clinton had a universe of faults but under her administration we likely wouldn't have seen married people being picked up and separated by border patrol. Health care, including Planned Parenthood, which is the only access to prenatal and gynecological health care many poor women have at all, wouldn't be at risk. The Paris Climate Accord wouldn't have been tossed out. We wouldn't be going the other way on mass incarceration, prison privatization and the drug war. We wouldn't be facing the rebirth of the *old* Jim Crow.

Which is not to say that a Clinton presidency would have meant peace and justice for all. It wouldn't have. She would have still pushed an agenda that elevated the American Empire in terrible ways. But the loss of even the most compromising of agreements, accords and legislation means that we are starting from negative numbers. It means that we can't focus on pushing for something far better than the ACA—like single-payer health care—but that we have to fight for even the most basic of rights.

At home, Future is looking at me, at America, sideways. They can't understand how we allowed this to happen. We have multiple discussions about the slave-era Electoral College, which privileges a minority of people when it comes to electing a person to the highest office in the land. We very seriously broach the idea of moving to Toronto, which a year before had elected not only Trump's polar opposite, Justin Trudeau, but a person far, far better than the candidate the Democratic party put up.

Because along with the horrors our communities face, we, as organizers, face real and imminent threats. As soon as he is inaugurated, Trump not only removes any vestige of the nods toward human rights that Obama had erected, but he says very specifically that he will have zero tolerance for we who are demanding police and law enforcement accountability, that his administration will be "a law and order administration . . . [and end the] dangerous anti-police atmosphere in America."

As of this writing, three of the organizers from Ferguson, DeAndre Joshua, Darren Seals and Edward Crawford, have all been found shot dead in their cars. The cars of two of the young men, DeAndre and Darren, were burned, which destroyed forensic evidence, and Edward's death was ruled a suicide—even as he had just started a new job and had secured a new apartment, hardly the action of someone looking to die.

Alicia, Opal and I have been sued by a right-winger who claims we instigated riots. Under Obama—because the lawsuit was filed while 44 was in office—we were not worried. Under 45 and Jeff Sessions, we are not so sure what will happen.

So yes, yes it is a terrifying time, as an organizer, as a new mother and as the wife of an immigrant living in a Queer relationship, to be in this nation. And I say that to Future. And then I say, I can't leave the work here.

Future agrees.

We, Alicia, Opal and I, helped build a vibrant, national network of brave organizers and we can't abandon ship. I can't abandon ship. We are all doing work in our locales, and top of my own list in LA County is stopping the building of a $3.5 billion jail. When I am at my most terrified for my family, for my new baby, in the end what makes me stay is us.

We are a forgotten generation. Worse, we are a generation that has been written off. We've been written off by the drug war. We've been written off by the war on gangs. We've been written off by mass incarceration and criminalization. We've been written off by broken public schools and we've been written off by gentrification that keeps us out of the very neighborhoods we've helped build. We actually don't give a fuck about shiny, polished candidates. We care about justice. We care about bold leaders and actions. We care about human rights and common decency. So there is no other place for me to be but here, where I can continue to help bring that into existence.

I know that it was organizers who pulled us out of chattel slavery and Jim Crow, and it is organizers who are pulling us out of their twenty-first-century progeny, including racist and deadly policing practices. And I know that if we do what we are called to do, curate events and conversations that lead to actions that lead to decisions about how we should and would live, we will win.

Since Black Lives Matter was born in 2013 we have done some incredible work. We have built a decentralized movement that encourages and supports local leaders to name and claim the work that is needed in order to make their communities more just. This is monumentally difficult in a world that has made even activism a celebrity pursuit. But we have more than 20 chapters across the United States, in Canada and the UK, all autonomous but all connected and coordinated. We have centered and amplified the voices of those not only made most vulnerable but most unheard, even as they are on the front lines at every hour and in every space: Black women—*all* Black women.

We have created space for us to finally be unapologetic about who we are and what we need to be actually free, not partially free. We have made it so that we can stand in our unedited truth. Our presence in the streets was the bullhorn needed to underscore the push for Obama to use his clemency powers. He left office with the smallest federal prison population in a generation, something he was not originally on track to do. We demand that the ongoing push for police accountability be at last taken seriously. So many have called for it before us and we stand on their shoulders and yell so loudly it can no longer be ignored. We make everyday people feel part of a push for change. People like Sandra Bland. We open the doors and ask people who have not been paid attention to to join us. And we have brought healing to our movement, the ideas and practices that demonstrate that as we seek to care for communities, we must also care for ourselves.

Even still, there is so much work to do as we push to fight this presidency and stop its Jim Crow–era aggressions. We are working collaboratively to create sustainable rapid response networks to violence and ICE raids. But we are also deeply committed to building Black political power and supporting bold leadership like Chokwe Antar Lumumba's in Jackson, Mississippi, and Stacey Abrams's in Georgia. We are committed to working closely with Jessica Byrd of Three Point Strategies, the Washington, DC–based consulting firm that works at the intersection of electoral politics and social justice. We can elect Black women to office who are committed to advancing human-centered agendas, leaders who understand and honor the truth that real leadership must be earned, not appointed. Or stolen. Or arrogant.

Across our network, we are devoted to pushing for and realizing bail reform and, perhaps closest to my own heart, we are envisioning and creating a new movement culture in which we care for the humanity of the people we're fighting for *and with.*

Recognizing that we are working with—and many of us are, ourselves—some of the most traumatized people in the United States, the BLM network has health and wellness directors dedicated to ending toxicity in our own organizations. We have a responsibility to do better by people than simply telling them at the point of burnout to go rest and renew and then come back to the same toxicity that depleted them. We, Black people, die younger and more frequently from diseases we can avoid, and given that the rest of our culture seems hell-bent on attacking our immune systems, we have to do better. What kind of food are we serving at conferences? Are we providing time throughout the workday to get people up and moving? Are our organizations paying the least while demanding the most from people we know are too committed to say no or ask for more, to ask for what they need and deserve? Are we including restorative practices in our organizations so that when we struggle with one another, we don't devolve into petty gossip or backbiting—or outright lies? Are we creating through lines for different levels of skill sets, the ones that are brought to us by people who have been forced to live in cages for 10 years, 20 years? Are we pushing ourselves in each conversation we have to really imagine the world we want to live in, rather than beginning with the compromise position? Are we calling for the abolition of prisons, knowing that in so doing, we are also calling for real and comprehensive health care, including mental health care? Knowing that it means that food security and housing security—hell, clean damn water—must be a given, as restorative justice practices must be too?

For years, I've neglected my own health and caretaking. If I struggled with intimacy in my romances, I also struggled with it when it came to myself. I resolve, in the wake of the Trump presidency, to end that, too. I begin working out again, four times a week. I start cooking more. I am traveling less and spending time in prayer each day. And I include fun in my life, joy to counteract this hate-filled world. I go to the arcade with friends. I roller skate. I designate park days. It's the Gabriel in me, the Brignac in me.

And perhaps above all, I am intentional with my family, ensuring Future and I have time each week to just love on each other and grow in our love. We center this beautiful child I had long ago imagined and whom I am now watching grow, whom I am now helping to grow, who teaches me every day what is possible. And that what is possible is more than even I can imagine, because as much as I loved Shine before I ever met him, I could not have imagined the depth of that love, the unending expanse of it.

And if ever someone calls my child a terrorist, if they call any of the children in my life terrorists, I will hold my child, any child, close to me and I will explain that terrorism is being stalked and surveilled simply because you are alive. And terrorism is being put in solitary confinement and starved and beaten. And terrorism is not being able to feed your children despite working three jobs. And terrorism is not having a decent school or a place to play. I will tell them that what freedom looks like, what democracy looks like, is the push for and realization of justice, dignity and peace.

And I will say that to my precious Shine, or Malik, or Nisa, or Nina or any of the children and young people we cherish and lift up, that you are brilliant beings of light. You have the power to shape-shift not only yourselves but the whole of the world. You, each one, are endowed with gifts you don't even yet know, and you, each one, are what love and the possibility of a world in which our lives truly matter looks like.

acknowledgments

Invariably, writing acknowledgments seems to fall as the most difficult part of any book. There are so many who ensured that we arrived here, in this place, the story told as fully and authentically as possible. The fear of forgetting someone, of failing to properly recognize someone who has helped, looms large. Even still, we have to try and in so doing, we begin with our agents, Tanya McKinnon and Victoria Sanders and the incredible dream team at VSA whose love and constructive care ensured and guided us long before there was a proposal or a book or a title in place. But when those did come into view, there was no home better for them than the one Monique Patterson made for us at St. Martin's Press, where on any given day you can find the hardest-working and most talented people in publishing.

dream hampton, Denene Millner, Imani Wilson, Isaac Skelton and Letta Neely all read or helped with early versions of the proposal that would become this book. We are very grateful for their feedback, all of which was invaluable, as was Robin Templeton's, whose incredibly sharp proofreading eye ensured we turned in the cleanest copy. And above all, for Nisa Yasmine, the one true daughter, who read the entire manuscript with an eye far more mature than her 17 years. She is a gift to us and the world.

We are grateful to the members of our political family who support and stand with us, even when it's not easy. They include our colleagues at MomsRising, and Monifa Bandele in particular; at the National CARES Mentoring Movement, and the ever-generous and loving Susan L. Taylor; our Formerly Incarcerated and Convicted People's Movement family; our Drug Policy Alliance family, with special love to Kassandra Frederique, Tony Newman, Lynne Lyman, Judh Grandchamps, Laini Madhubuti, Chloe Cockburn, Dr. Carl Hunt and Deborah Small; and for Michelle Alexander who stood with us on faith, and whose scholarship informs us on a daily basis.

We are grateful to *Essence* magazine, in particular Patrik Henry Bass and Vanessa De Luca, for their work to ensure the first public telling of the birth of the Black Lives Matter movement.

We live in gratitude for the existence and work of Dignity and Power Now, the Malcolm X Grassroots Movement, the Strategy Center, the team at Blackbird, BYP100, Dream Defenders, Darnell Moore, Kirsten West Savali, Brittney Cooper, Malkia Cyril, Rosa Clemente, Marc Lamont Hill, Rashad Robinson, the St. Elmo's Village family, Reverend

Starsky Wilson, the Performers of Power from the Mouths of the Occupied, Law for Black Lives and the Movement for Black Lives.

There are individuals who, because of their various and incredible gifts and magnificent hearts, must be named: Carla Gonzalez, Mark Anthony Johnson, Quay Quay, Tanya Bernard, Cheeraz Gormon, Brittney Ferrell, Alexis Templeton, Damon Davis, Elle Hearns, Aaryn Lang, Lourdes Ashley Hunter, Donna Hill, Vitaly, Ariane White, Sean Sparks, Richard Edmond, Melina Abdullah, Nora Alexis, Everton Brown, Lavon Leak Wilkes, Monica Dennis, Mercedes Chambliss, Piper Kerman, Lateefah Simon, Francisca Porchas, Esperanza Martinez, Kelly Archbold and Noni Limar.

We do this work today because on another day work was done by Assata Shakur, Angela Davis, Miss Major, the Black Panther Party, the members of the Black Arts Movement, SNCC, the RNA, Malcolm X, Martin Luther King, Ella Baker and so many others. We owe you and the world a debt of gratitude.

And first, last and always, our love and gratitude is without end for Alicia Garza, Opal Tometi, the leaders and members of the more than 40 chapters of BLM across the globe and the staff of the Black Lives Matter Global Network, Shanelle Matthews, Nikita Mitchell, Kandace Montgomery, Miski Noor, Prentis Hemphill, Whitney Washington, Rodney Diverlus and Rhiana Anthony.

We believe we will be free.